POETRY AND PROPHECY

Buryat Shaman (*back view*)

POETRY & PROPHECY

BY

N. KERSHAW CHADWICK

*Fellow of Newnham College,
Cambridge*

CAMBRIDGE
AT THE UNIVERSITY PRESS
1952

CAMBRIDGE UNIVERSITY PRESS
Cambridge, New York, Melbourne, Madrid, Cape Town,
Singapore, São Paulo, Delhi, Tokyo, Mexico City

Cambridge University Press
The Edinburgh Building, Cambridge CB2 8RU, UK

Published in the United States of America by
Cambridge University Press, New York

www.cambridge.org
Information on this title: www.cambridge.org/9781107689510

© Cambridge University Press 1942

This publication is in copyright. Subject to statutory exception
and to the provisions of relevant collective licensing agreements,
no reproduction of any part may take place without the written
permission of Cambridge University Press.

First published 1942
Reprinted 1952
First paperback edition 2011

A catalogue record for this publication is available from the British Library

ISBN 978-1-107-68951-0 Paperback

Cambridge University Press has no responsibility for the persistence or
accuracy of URLs for external or third-party internet websites referred to in
this publication, and does not guarantee that any content on such websites is,
or will remain, accurate or appropriate.

To

THE PROPHETS AND POETS
of other Continents, whose Spiritual Vision and Art
has been perfected and transmitted
from generation to generation
without the aid of writing

I DEDICATE THIS

LITTLE BOOK

CONTENTS

PREFACE *page* xi

CHAPTER

I Poetic Inspiration and the Trance of the Seer: The Evidence of Early Europe *page* 1

II The Trance of the Seer: The Evidence of Modern Oral Literature *page* 15

III Inspiration: The Seer's Call, and his Artistic and Spiritual Gifts *page* 41

IV The Mantic Technique and the Artificial Regulation of Ecstasy *page* 58

V Ritual and Magic, and their Relationship to the Mantic Tradition *page* 73

VI The Spiritual Journeys of the Seer *page* 90

INDEX *page* 106

ILLUSTRATIONS

Buryat Shaman; back view		*frontispiece*
1. Buryat Shaman; front view	*to face page*	62
2. Buryat Shaman in ecstasy, and wearing bird costume	,,	64
3. Oirot Horse Sacrifice	,,	76
4. Temple Buildings, Kyzyl, Chinese Turkestan	,,	82
5. Etruscan Tomb Painting of the Dead	,,	88
6. Dramatic Presentation of Yama, God of the Dead, from Choni in the Chinese Province of Kansu	,,	92
7. Yama and attendant Demons in a Mystery Play from Choni in the Chinese Province of Kansu	,,	100

PREFACE

Poetry and Prophecy are the expression of human thought at its most intense and concentrated moments, stimulated by excitement, and expressed in artistic form. Prophecy is the expression of thought, whether subjective or objective, and of knowledge, whether of the present, the future, or the past, which has been acquired by inspiration, and which is uttered in a condition of exaltation or trance, or couched in the traditional form of such utterances. Poetry, it has been said, is the record of the happiest and best moments of the best and happiest lives.

The nature and record of thought uttered in moments of exalted vision, and its form of expression and transmission, are important subjects worthy of investigation. What is it precisely which dictates the form of Man's spiritual visions? How and why do we communicate them to our fellow men? How and why do we sometimes endeavour to give more or less permanent form to our thoughts?

The answer to these questions can only be found when we have before us the results of wide investigation among peoples of the present and the past. To understand the individual experience we must know the experience of others. Comparative work is essential, and the wider the field of comparison the better. The experience of exclusively literate communities is too narrow. The vast majority of mankind are not literate. The object of this little book is to stimulate interest in the mental culture, and more especially in the history of thought, and its

PREFACE

expression in literary (oral) form, among peoples who have no writing, or whose writing is confined to a small lettered class, and whose writing materials are scarce, such as vellums.

The first qualification for such a study must be a wholesome humility. The knowledge of writing, and the ease and swiftness with which knowledge can be transmitted by this means, have sometimes obscured the intellectual achievements of peoples in a less advanced stage of material culture. An immediate corrective is, of course, to be found in the study of Asiatic thought. This will readily be conceded in view of the ancient culture and written literature of the countries of Central, Southern, and Eastern Asia. But it is less readily apprehended in regard to Africa, whose achievements in spiritual matters are still very imperfectly recognised. The intellectual attainments of the South Sea Islanders are probably higher than those of any other people ignorant of the art of writing, and have astonished all those who have made themselves acquainted with them.

The disproportionate importance which has been attached to writing has also obscured the wealth of traditional thought which has been transmitted from past times among peoples on the periphery of our more advanced civilisations. Lack of respect and sympathy for the leaders of native thought, and ignorance of the language in which it is expressed, have allowed much of the past and present mental culture of unlettered communities to perish unrecorded. The loss is essentially ours, and until we have recaptured this it is impossible for us to realise the close relationship of one class of spiritual thinkers to another, and the traditional character of their imagery. For us who live in a Christian community the need for intellectual humility is especially pressing. If it

PREFACE xiii

be said that our greatest prophet and spiritual teacher is essentially a great Seer or Shaman, it would not be in any sense to detract from the greatness of Christ, but only to place other seers and shamans in their right proportion, and historical relationship to Him.

If the history of thought among backward and unlettered communities is worthy of serious study, it follows that their medium of expression, and the transmission of thought through long periods of time, and over wide areas, is equally worthy of investigation. Where all the volumes in the library of spiritual thought must be carried in the memory, they will be found to be usually composed in poetry. Hence it is that the study of thought, and the study of poetry, current among unlettered peoples, are inseparable.

But we must not expect minute exactitude in the transmission of thought and knowledge, whether of divine or secular matters, when these are handed down through the medium of poetry. Where the medium of transmission, the oral book, is a human being, the subjective element plays a preponderant part. The thought and the expression are coloured by the mood of the moment. Inspiration is as important as memory, and inspiration, according to its degree, governs the form in which the thought is couched. Over a wide area of the earth poetry and prophecy are the two essential elements in the co-ordination and synthesis of thought and its transmission.

It is hoped that this little book may help to extend interest in, and to create a more sympathetic attitude towards the leaders of thought, the prophetic poets, or 'mantic' persons of unlettered communities. And here a word should be said on the use of the word 'mantic' in the following pages. The word 'mantic' has been preferred to 'prophetic' for two reasons: firstly because the latter word has come to be limited, at least in ordinary usage, to declarations relating to the future, whereas the former can refer to the (commonly unknown) present and past, just as much as to the future; and secondly because 'prophetic' is generally used of *declarations* of knowledge obtained by revelation or from some inner light, whereas 'mantic' may be used just as well for the *possession* or *cultivation* as for the *declaration* of knowledge.

The nucleus of this book consists of three papers read before the Anthropological Section of the British Association in 1937, 1938, and 1939. It is intended primarily to be suggestive, and to direct interest towards some fresh fields of study. It does not aim at deploying, still less at exhausting, the evidence in any field. It is, however, only the brief and condensed expression of the conclusions to which the writer has been brought by a prolonged collection and examination of material, much of which she has published elsewhere. If, therefore, some of these conclusions appear somewhat bold in so slender a volume, it may be mentioned here that they represent conclusions which have been arrived at as the result of twenty years' research in oral literature.

The most important conclusion to which this research points is that among unlettered and backward peoples spiritual thought and its expression are largely of a traditional character, derived ultimately from the great centres of civilisation. Like ripples made by pebbles cast into a pond, the waves of culture spread outwards from the great cultures of the past—Mesopotamia, Egypt, Etruria, Greece, China; and again, in more recent periods—Rome, Persia, Arabia, India, Turkestan. The ripples from the great centres of culture grow fainter as they spread towards the circumference, and they intermingle with other ripples formed by other culture centres from the past and present. New centres of activity and diffusion are started by such contacts. But the elements of the new cultures thus formed are only new combinations of the elements derived from great cultures. The evidence of oral literature suggests that poor and backward communities are capable of transmitting, combining, adapting, and perfecting inherited culture, but not of originating new ideas. They are the oral libraries of the world's ancient cultures.

But the study of oral literature points to yet another important conclusion. Similar ideas and literary forms which may be found in areas far apart cannot be regarded as of independent origin. Wherever their history can be traced, step by step, it can be shown that their immediate forerunners are derived from common cultures nearer to a common centre in the past, rather than from 'primitive' origins. The study of oral tradition urges us to substitute history for speculation; to abandon the assumption that the culture of the most backward communities of the present day bears any relationship to that of truly 'primitive', or early man. If we are content to work humbly, and retrace the history of our peripheral cultures by means only of known facts, it will, I think, become clear that the farther back we can carry our researches the higher the culture becomes, and the more the immediate sources of these cultures tend to converge. In our present stage of knowledge it is not always possible to find the centre from which a ripple has radiated. The rapid succession of cults and cultures over a long period of time may have effaced all traces. It is part of the value of the oral traditions and culture of communities on the outer edge of the World that they have preserved for us, not the primitive experiments of early man, but re-

xvi PREFACE

flections of the long forgotten spiritual life and art of the great civilisations of the past.

My thanks are due to Mr J. M. de Navarro who brought to my notice many years ago the pictures of Buryat Shamans reproduced in this book from the *Berliner Illustrirte Zeitung*; and also to Professor and Mrs Ure who brought me a fine collection of photographs of Etruscan tomb paintings from Italy, one of which I have published here. The pictures of the Dramatic Presentation of Yama, the God of the Dead, and of Yama and attendant Demons, from a Mystery Play in Choni in the Chinese province of Kansu are from photographs by Dr Rock of Yunnan. The picture of the Temple Buildings, Kyzyl, Chinese Turkestan, is reproduced from A. von Le Coq's *Buried Treasures of Chinese Turkestan*, translated by Anna Barwell from German and published by Messrs Allen and Unwin (London, 1928). Le Coq's book was first published in German in 1926 under the title "Auf Hellas Spuren in Ostturkistan".

In conclusion I wish to express my thanks to the Syndics of the University Press for publishing this book, and to the Staff for the careful manner in which they have carried out the printing and the corrections.

N. KERSHAW CHADWICK

CAMBRIDGE
AUGUST 1941

ACKNOWLEDGEMENT

Thanks are due to J. C. Hinrichs Verlag, Leipzig—Gotha, for permission to reproduce Plate 4.

CHAPTER I

POETIC INSPIRATION AND THE TRANCE OF THE SEER: THE EVIDENCE OF EARLY EUROPE

Our first task in considering the relationship between poetry and manticism is to think away our modern ideas of poetry. In the greater part of the Ancient World, poetry was not a thing to be read, but to be heard, and to be heard by as many people as possible. This was the only form of publication. And so oral poetry was not generally recited, but rather sung or chanted. Poetry is fundamentally connected with music, especially vocal music. Instrumental accompaniment is not essential, and is often absent.

Where the art of extempore poetical composition is widely practised, the form of poetry often lacks rigidity. The distinction between prose and poetry is sometimes not very clearly marked, and often seems to be dependent on the presence or absence of the musical element. But wherever there is music there is rhythm, and a certain degree of artificial arrangement and length of phrase. Always with chanted speech there is polish and artificial diction. Tradition soon overlays it with formulae. In general it may be said that poetry in its simplest form is polished speech or eloquence, governed by musical standards.

The earliest Greek poets attribute their poetic gifts

directly to the Muses. The Homeric poems contain several invocations to the Muse. The *Odyssey* opens with these words:

> Tell me, O Muse, etc.

In the same poems minstrels are said to have received their inspiration from them. Hesiod makes a much more ambitious claim. He declares that when he received his inspiration from the Muses, who taught him poetry as he was keeping his sheep on the slopes of Helicon, they inspired him with a voice to celebrate both the future and the past. Similarly in the *Iliad* (1. 70) Calchas, the seer of the Achaeans, is said to know the present, the future, and the past. These are important statements, for the celebration of the past implies knowledge. The name of the mother of the Muses is 'Memory'. The poems composed by Hesiod in response to his gift of inspiration are largely of a learned and didactic character. An early Greek story of a contest between two seers (Calchas and Mopsos) attributes the victory to Mopsos because he knew the number of figs on a certain tree. In Tatar oral poetry we find a similar contest between two sages with mantic gifts, whose knowledge consists in similar pedantic natural history.

> The stars of Heaven they enumerated,
> The fish of the sea they enumerated,
> The flowers of the earth they enumerated,
> The peoples of the earth they enumerated,
> The trees shone upon by the moon they enumerated,
> The stones shone upon by the sun they enumerated.

In this contest, however, both the sages are surpassed by a woman who knows seven words more than either of them.[1] The claim of the Greek seers to knowledge of the past through inspiration is, indeed, attributed equally by the Tatars in their oral literature to their seers or shamans. In a story recorded by the Swedish ethnographer Castrén, a certain Kögel-Khan says of himself: 'I am a shaman, who knows the future, the past, and everything which is taking place in the present, both above and below the earth.'[2]

The earliest evidence known to me for the gift of poetry as the immediate result of divine inspiration in our own country comes from the Venerable Bede.[3] In describing monastic life at Whitby[4] under the Abbess Hild, who died in 680, Bede tells us that it was the custom in the evening for the villagers to pass the harp round, and sing to it in turn; but Caedmon, who had never been able to learn a song, used quietly to leave the gathering, as he saw the harp approaching him. One night, as he was in the byre attending to the cattle, an angel appeared to him and commanded him to sing; and immediately his lips were unsealed, and he sang our earliest recorded Saxon religious poem. From that moment Caedmon became a great composer of religious poetry.

But at this period the divine voice grows silent. Anglo-Saxon literary records give us no further reason to believe that either the poets or the prose writers among our Saxon forefathers made the ambitious claim attributed to the humble Caedmon by Bede. King Alfred's thoughts dwell

[1] Radlov, *Proben der Volkslitteratur der Türkischen Stämme Süd-Sibiriens*, vol. I (St Petersburg, 1866), p. 202.
[2] Castrén, *Nordische Reisen und Forschungen*, ed. Schiefner, vol. IV (St Petersburg, 1857), p. 256.
[3] *Hist. Eccles.* IV, 24.
[4] The word is *Streoneshealh*, which is generally identified with Whitby.

on secular learning, laboriously acquired with the help of Grimbold his mass-priest and Asser his bishop. The anonymous composers of *Beowulf* and the poets in the Exeter Book speak as they have been taught by other minstrels. The minstrel in *Beowulf*, in reciting the story of Beowulf's adventure, recites not by a divine gift, but as one who 'remembered things of very long ago', and who was accomplished in the skilled use of artificial poetic diction; but nothing is said of a divine origin of his art. We have *The Dream of the Cross*, which is believed to be in the early tradition; but here the literary convention is that of a dream, and the poem is composed in the style characteristic of general medieval religious thought rather than in the style of native traditional prophecy. The absence of any claim to divine inspiration is especially surprising in the case of Cynewulf, whose poetry is concerned exclusively with ecclesiastical subjects, and whose artistic life was devoted to presenting Biblical and hagiological tradition to his fellow-men in the artistic form of their ancient heroic poems. Cynewulf[1] might well have claimed the gift of God; but he is silent on the subject. We have no evidence that Caedmon had any successors.

It would seem not improbable that Caedmon was the end of the Celtic rather than the beginning of the Saxon tradition. We hear of British poets who were famous at the Court of Maelgwn, in the sixth century. Two of the most important were Taliesin and Talhaern, the latter surnamed *Tat aguen* (i.e. *Tad awen*),[2] 'Father of poetry',

1 See, however, Kennedy, *Poems of Cynewulf* (London, 1910), p. 126.
2 The expression occurs in the *Black Book of Carmarthen*, ed. Skene, *Four Ancient Books of Wales* (Edinburgh, 1868), XIX, 10 (Str. 4).

THE TRANCE OF THE SEER

or of poetic inspiration. The same expression is used of Tydain in the Welsh *Triads*,[1] of whom it is added in explanation: 'Who first made an art of song, and regulated inspiration.' To the poet Taliesin tradition has ascribed a large quantity of poetry of the kind which is associated elsewhere with the intellectual and mantic class—with the *filid* like Amargin, and with mantic kings like Mongan in Ireland. There is good reason to believe that this mantic poetry was already flourishing in both Wales and Ireland in the seventh century.[2] From the latter country we have a considerable amount of oral mantic literature recorded from the early eighth century onwards, while there seems good ground for believing that Taliesin was a historical figure of the sixth century.[3]

This early Celtic literature, recorded in MSS. from oral tradition, is a great unexploited field for the student of prophetic inspiration. From both Wales and Ireland we have life-histories of mantic persons, composed in saga form, and a rich wealth of poetry attributed to seers and sages, which claims to have been recited by them during their periods of inspiration.[4] Probably no other literature offers such a wealth of material for differentiating between various types of manticism, and various classes

1 *Triads*, III, 92 (*Myvyrian Archaeology*, p. 409; see Chadwick, *The Growth of Literature*, vol. I (Cambridge, 1932), pp. 637, 664).
2 See Chadwick, *Growth*, vol. I, p. 468 f.
3 According to Sir John Morris Jones, there can be no reasonable doubt that Taliesin is a historical figure of the sixth century who flourished about the time of Maelgwn—the period to which tradition also points. See *Y Cymmrodor*, vol. XXVIII, p. 151.
4 How far these poems were actually composed by the seers and on the occasions to which they are attributed matters little. The consistency of the literary forms and formulae, and the early date of much of the evidence, speaks strongly in favour of the substantial veracity of the literary tradition.

of mantic persons, such as the *druid, fili, geilt, awenyddion*, to mention only a few. Celtic literature, moreover, is particularly rich in information relating to the more technical side of manticism, the signs by which the youthful sage is recognised in early life, the youthful education and upbringing of the seer, his rule of life and professional dress and accessories, his ascetic training and preparation for his calling. More important still are the stories which tell of his later spiritual experiences—his adventures in the spirit world, the various stages through which his spirit passes to its divine vision. Hardly less interesting are the accounts, often fragmentary and obscure, but strangely consistent, of the seer's technique for bringing himself into the inspired condition. We note the preliminary period of seclusion, the stimulating food and drink, the necessity of absence of distraction, the assistance rendered by his companions.[1] These and all other elements in the mantic process and the mantic experience are described with a wealth of technical terminology which proves that among the early Celtic peoples the inculcation of poetic inspiration and the entire mantic art were developed and elaborated to a degree for which we know no parallel. It is particularly in regard to this mantic technique and the intimacy and completeness with which the mantic experience during ecstasy is described that Celtic literature is deserving of careful study by students of inspiration and of trance.

Norse literature is only less rich than Irish in sidelights on early mantic belief and practice, and serves to link the manticism of the islands off the Atlantic coast of Europe

[1] I have treated some aspects of Celtic manticism in greater detail in several articles of *Scottish Gaelic Studies*, vols. IV–VII (1934, 1935).

THE TRANCE OF THE SEER

with the shamanism of the great Asiatic continent. Here we find ample indications that Teutonic no less than Celtic manticism was deliberately regulated—which is equivalent to saying that it was a long-established and highly-honoured practice. Thus we learn that when Halfdan the Black, the father of Harold the Fair-haired,[1] king of Norway, wished to obtain a mantic vision, by the advice of a seer named Thorleifr the Wise, he went to sleep in a pig-stye,[2] which is undoubtedly a barrow. From the *Hallfrethar Saga*, ch. 6, we learn that Thorleifr the Wise, or more properly 'the Seer',[3] a namesake and descendant of the latter, also sat on a barrow, and had mantic dreams. Similarly in str. 42 of the early Norse poem known as the *Völuspá*, 'The Prophecy of the *völva*, or Seeress', a certain Eggthér, who is described as *gýgjar hirthir*, 'the keeper of the witch', sits on a mound and plucks his harp strings. We may refer to an interesting Runic inscribed monument[4] from Snoldelev, Denmark, dating probably from the early ninth century, which is said to commemorate Gunnwald, the son of Hróaldr, the *thulr* ('seer') at Sal*haug*ar. The word *haugr* means 'barrow'. It will be seen that the association of the mantic vision with the dead is generally recognised in early Norse literature. Welsh tradition[5] recognises the

[1] King Harold's traditional dates are 860–930.
[2] See the early Norse collection of stories by Snorri Sturluson (who lived in the early thirteenth century) known as the *Heimskringla* (*Saga of Halfdan the Black*, ch. VII).
[3] The epithet *spaki*, used of Thorleifr, implies supernatural knowledge as well as great sagacity.
[4] L. F. A. Wimmer, *Danske Runemindesmærker* (Copenhagen and Christiania, 1914), p. 99.
[5] See the first story in the collection of medieval Welsh prose stories known as the *Mabinogion*, translated into English by Lady Charlotte Guest.

same association. In a Welsh medieval saga the hero Pwyll obtains a mantic experience by sitting on a mound.

The evidence of early Norse literature for the actual functional value of the use of combined music and poetry by the seer is particularly full and instructive. In the *Thorfinns Saga Karlsefnis* (ch. 3) the seeress who is called in to give an oracle insists that she cannot get the spirits to attend to her until she can get a singer *with a good voice* to chant the required spells (*galdrar*). Eventually a girl is found who is actually a Christian, but who has learnt the spells in her youth. She sings unwillingly, but her voice is good, and the spells are the right ones, and so her singing proves quite effective, and the seeress is able to give her oracle. It is interesting to note that it is not the seeress herself who is the singer of the spells. Her own inspiration comes from the music and words sung by another. The spirits come in definite response to word and music, and no other compelling power is needed. Again in *Laxdaela Saga* (ch. 37), when Kotkell and his accomplices are working even harmful magic, known as *seithr*, the beauty of their singing is especially commented on. In the same way we find that the oral literature of the Tatars is full of references to the power of music to reach, to move, and even to summon spirits. It is of itself efficacious to raise the dead, i.e. to recall the wandering soul to the empty body.

The word used for spells in early Norse is *galdrar* (sing. *galdr*). *Galdrar* are always chanted (*gala*) on such occasions. In the historical sagas the harp is unknown, though it is found in poetry, as we have seen, and—rarely—in the legendary sagas, where its associations are distinctly mantic. In the legendary story of Nornagestr, which has been incorporated in the longer *Saga of Olaf Tryggvason*

THE TRANCE OF THE SEER 9

contained in the *Flateyjarbók*, Nornagestr himself, who clearly came from a supernatural region (*Ódáinsakr*,[1] 'the land of immortals' ruled by a certain King Guthmundr), is an accomplished harpist and poet. So also in the *Saga of Herrauthr and Bósi*, Bósi plays his harp in the hall of this same King Guthmundr. But in the historical sagas poetry is always sung without accompaniment. The importance attached to music is illustrated in *Örvar-Odds Saga* (ch. 2), where we read of a seeress Heithr who is accompanied on her visits by a troop of fifteen boys and fifteen girls. They play no part in the scene in which Heithr delivers her prophecies, but in one text they are described as *raddlith*, which probably means 'choir', (literally, 'singing company').

The important part played by mantic accessories in regulated inspiration is emphasised in early Norse literature. We hear of the *seith-stafr* or wand, the special hat,[2] and the cloak, such as are worn by the 'little Völva'[3] in *Thorfinns Saga*, and by the god Othin; the mantic gloves of Thor, of the little Völva, and of characters who visit

[1] This is not actually stated in the saga itself; but the juxtaposition of the *tháttr af Nornagesti* and the *tháttr Helga Thórissonar*, and the obvious connection of the stories which they contain, makes this clear. *Heithr* appears to be a common name or title of a seeress. See *Landnámabók*, III, 2; *Örvar-Odds Saga*, ch. 2; *Hrólfs Saga Kraka*, ch. 3; *Völuspá*, str. 22; *Hyndluljóth*, str. 34. *Heithr* is also the name of the foster-mother of King Harold the Fair-haired (see p. 7 above), who lived in the neighbourhood of the White Sea (see the *Saga of Olaf Tryggvason, Flateyjarbók*, ch. 467). For further instances see A. Olrik, 'At Sidde på Höj', *Danske Studier* (1909), p. 1 ff.

[2] We may compare the Welsh and Irish so-called 'bardic hat' and the cloak of the Irish *filid*.

[3] The unexplained epithet 'little' applied to the seeress in the saga is puzzling. I know nothing exactly parallel in Norse. Can it possibly be interpreted in the light of the Yakut shamans who, according to Sieroszewski (*Revue de l'Histoire des Religions*, vol. XVI, 1902, p. 628) are divided into three classes: the Great Shaman; the Middling

Ódáinsakr; the high boots—again worn by the 'little Völva' and by Othin—in fact a regular shaman's outfit. No drum is mentioned, though, as we have seen, music is of great importance. Othin's chief mantic accessory is a preserved human head which he is in the habit of consulting as an oracle. Mantic heads are unknown in Norse historical tradition, though they figure prominently in the Irish saga of the Battle of Allen, which relates to the year 722. In Norse sagas of *Ódáinsakr* we read of prophetic heads stuck on the end of drinking-horns—perhaps reminiscent of the prophetic mead of Norse mythology.

The most interesting figure in Norse mantic tradition is that of the God Othin. He is *fjölkunnigr*, 'extremely knowing', with the implication of supernatural knowledge, and he is gifted with the power of shape-changing. He is the *thulr* of the gods, the inspired poet and seer, as well as the giver of poetic inspiration and of mantic wisdom. His name, *Othin*, *Wod-en*, has been thought to mean 'an inspired person'. He has something in common with the Irish god Manannán mac Lír, as has the cult of Othin with that of the Irish belief in *Tír na n-Óg*, the 'Land of the Young', and *Tír Tairngaire*, the 'Land of Promise', or rather of 'Prophetic Inspiration'; but his most obvious affinities are with the Siberian shamans whom he resembles in a remarkable degree. He is, in fact, the divine shaman of the Norse pantheon, and his affinities are to be sought in northern Asia.

_{Shaman; the Little Shaman. It is to be suspected that some such conception also lies behind the curious and equally unexplained titles *Hár* ('High', 'sublime'), *Jafnhár* ('Equally lofty', or 'of medium sublimity') and *Thrithi* ('Third') applied to the three 'wise' beings interviewed by the traveller in the early Norse prose work *Gylfaginning*.}

THE TRANCE OF THE SEER

The manticism of Europe goes back to early times. The Greek evidence is too well known to need recalling here, and relates not only to the oracular responses of the Pythia, recorded in poetical form by the Delphic priests, but also to Thrace, where manticism appears to have been highly cultivated.[1] In both Greece and Thrace the preoccupations of mantic persons appear to have been concerned to a considerable extent with antiquarian studies,[2] while the Thracian seers were also interested in natural philosophy and speculative theology.[3] In these features they have much in common with the mantic classes of ancient Gaul.

Among the ancient Gauls the mantic class was evidently of great importance and held in the highest esteem. These mantic persons seem to have consisted chiefly of men; but prophetesses were not unknown. The evidence regarding the mantic class as a whole is somewhat difficult to unravel, owing to the confusion which seems to have existed among Roman writers between the functions of bards, seers (*vates*, *manteis*), and druids; but it is clear that the prophetic function was held in high esteem. It is stated by Cicero[4] that one of the chief druids who was personally known to him, Diviciacus by name, claimed to have the power of foretelling the future. Among their many intellectual preoccupations, antiquarian studies[5] and natural philosophy formed important elements, along with speculations on the future

[1] See especially Herodotus, IV, 96.
[2] Jordanes, *Get.* 5 ff.
[3] Jordanes, *loc. cit.*; Herodotus, *loc. cit.* For a fuller discussion of this subject, see Chadwick, *Growth*, vol. I, pp. 643 ff.
[4] *De Divin.* I, 41.
[5] Ammianus Marcellinus, XV, ix, 4.

life. Their educational system, which was singularly elaborated, was carried on chiefly in the form of traditional poems, orally transmitted.[1] The nearest affinities of the Gaulish intellectual classes are with the Brahmins of India, to whom in many respects they bear a close resemblance, notably in their educational system, the nature of their speculations, their forest life (doubtless for the sake of seclusion), their attention to traditional oral literature.[2] The resemblances are so close that they can hardly have been fortuitous. The Thracians, it will be remembered, marched with Teutonic peoples on the north and with Celtic peoples on the west. It is tempting to suppose that they may have formed a link in early times between the ancient mantic systems of the southern portions of *Eurasia*, as the cult of Othin and other features of Norse religion bear witness to an ancient link between Teutonic and Celtic manticism on the one hand and the shamanism of northern Asia on the other. In this connection we must not overlook the apparently close connection between the Gaulish Druids and the oak sanctuaries of the Lithuanians and the Old Prussians.[3] The religious system of the latter, as described by Matthaeus Praetorius,[4] who wrote *c.* 1670–80, with its educational system and concentration on antiquarian matters, seems to have had much in common with that of the Druids.

In considering the antiquity and affinities of manticism in ancient Europe, the importance of the linguistic

[1] Caesar, *Gall.* VI, 13 f.
[2] For a fuller comparison see Chadwick, *Growth*, vol. II, p. 614.
[3] See Dottin, *Antiquité Celtique* (Paris, 1915), p. 389 f. The most important evidence comes from Jordanes, *loc. cit.* See further the philological evidence cited by Chadwick, *Growth*, vol. I, p. 611, footnote 1.
[4] See *Deliciae Prussicae* (Extracts, ed. by W. Pierson, Berlin, 1871), p. 24.

evidence should not be overlooked. Certain words are common to both the Teutonic and Celtic languages. The word *geilt*, used of a certain type of ascetic recluse who has received a vision in battle, is identical in Norse and Irish, and may therefore be taken as a recent borrowing (by the former from the latter); but such words as Norse *seithr*, Welsh *hud*, Lith. *saitas*, which are of common origin, have passed through various sound-changes, have had a long independent history in the various languages, and have come to bear different technical significances in the different languages. Thus in Norse the expression 'to make *seithr*' has a practical significance, and implies not only divining the future, but also—at least to some extent —controlling it. To practise *seithr* is an elaborate process, in which, as we have seen, the beauty of the singing is emphasised as an important element. Lithuanian *saitas*, on the other hand, denotes 'the interpretation of signs'. In medieval Welsh saga *hud* is used in reference to witchcraft, and the art of the magician. But in Welsh *hud-lath*, in Norse *seith-stafr*, both denote the magician's wand. The most interesting of the words common to the Celtic and Teutonic languages are the Welsh *gwawd*, AS. *wōþ-*, ON. *óthr*, 'poetry', 'eloquence', and their derivatives. These Welsh words are closely related to L. *vates*, while the name of the god, AS. *Woden*, ON. *Óthinn*, is probably related both to these words and to AS. *wōd*, N. *óthr*, 'frenzied', 'mad'. We may compare also N. *Óthrerir*, the name of the mythical vessel in which the mead of poetic inspiration was kept. The word was doubtless applied originally to the mead itself, and means 'that which stimulates to poetry or eloquence'.[1]

[1] For a further discussion of these terms, see Chadwick, *Growth*, vol. 1, p. 620.

From this brief survey it is clear that the function of the seer was practically universal in early Europe. For centuries before Christ it was important in the south—in Thrace, in Greece, and doubtless in Etruria. During the Roman period and the Dark Ages it was held in high estimation in central Europe. Long before the close of the first millennium it had left a rich store of legend to the Celtic and Teutonic populations of the outer fringes of Europe.

The fundamental elements of the prophetic function seem to have been everywhere the same. Everywhere the gift of poetry is inseparable from divine inspiration. Everywhere this inspiration carries with it knowledge—whether of the past, in the form of history and genealogy; of the hidden present, in the form commonly of scientific information; and of the future, in the form of prophetic utterance in the narrower sense. Always this knowledge is uttered in poetry which is accompanied by music, whether of song or instrument. Music is everywhere the medium of communication with spirits. Invariably we find that the poet and seer attributes his inspiration to contact with supernatural powers, and his mood during prophetic utterance is exalted and remote from that of his normal existence. Generally we find that a recognised process is in vogue by which the prophetic mood can be induced at will. The lofty claims of the poet and seer are universally admitted, and he himself holds a high status wherever he is found. In addition to all this we find a common vocabulary of technical terms which goes back to early times.

CHAPTER II

THE TRANCE OF THE SEER: THE EVIDENCE OF MODERN ORAL LITERATURE

In some respects our information regarding the seers of modern times in the more backward parts of Asia and Africa and Polynesia is less intimate and satisfactory, coming as it does for the most part from observers of alien race and more 'modern', or 'advanced', or 'civilised' outlook. The involuntary attitude of the recorder is bound to be unsympathetic in the nature of things, and so, in the nature of things, largely uncomprehending. The Celtic and Teutonic records, made by people of the same language and traditions as those of the people to whom they relate, should be of great help in guiding us to an understanding of similar phenomena on the great Eurasian continent, of which our Celtic and Teutonic forefathers occupied the peninsulas and outermost islands in early times. But the most important source of information for the manticism of to-day must always be the oral literature of the people who still practise manticism, and especially the utterances of the seers themselves.

Among the peoples of northern Siberia[1] the seer, or shaman as the seer is generally called,[2] is probably the

1 I am greatly indebted to Miss E. J. Lindgren for bringing to my notice, as well as for lending me, some of the more recent books and articles relating to shamans referred to in the following pages.
2 The name varies among different peoples. Among the Altai Tatars he is known as a *kam*. 'Shaman' is said to be a Tungus word. See Laufer, 'The Origin of the Word *Shaman*', *American Anthropologist* (N.S.), vol. XIX, no. 3 (1917), pp. 361 ff.

most important person in the community. Among the shaman's functions that of 'prophesying' or speaking on religious subjects in an exalted condition of mind approximating to a trance is one of the most important. To what extent the shaman is actually in a dissociated condition during these manifestations of his 'power' is one of the questions chiefly exercising the minds of ethnologists at the present time. In the form of shamanism practised among the Altai Tatars the intellectual element is important, while the artistic form of the *kamlanie*, as the performance is called, is developed to an astonishing degree. Among the most interesting of these performances is the journey of the shaman, in spirit, to conduct the communal sacrifice to Heaven on behalf of his tribe,[1] or to conduct the souls of the dead to the Underworld.[2] In the annual sacrifice the shaman by song and action represents himself as making a journey with the sacrificial horse through a successive series of superimposed Heavens, pausing in each *oloh* or stage of his journey and indicating to his audience the topography of this particular 'Heaven', and the incidents in which he is taking part. The number of Heavens scaled by the shaman depends upon his powers. Very few are able to reach the highest Heaven. The illusion is created by a kind of religious ballet, in which the shaman is the sole performer, and which consists of a combination of dance, song, and

[1] For a detailed description of the ceremony among the Tatars of the Altai, see Radlov, *Aus Sibirien*, vol. II (Leipzig, 1884), p. 19 ff. See also Hildén, 'Om Shamanismen i Altai', *Terra, Geografiska Föreningens Tidskrift*, vol. XXVIII (1916), pp. 138 ff.
[2] Radlov, *op. cit.* p. 52. Further references to such journeys among the Tatars and other Siberian peoples have been cited by me in vol. LXVI, p. 308 f. of the *Journal of the Royal Anthropological Institute*.

EVIDENCE OF MODERN ORAL LITERATURE 17

extempore poetry, together with a considerable amount of mimesis. Performances resembling more or less closely those of the Tatar shaman's journey to Heaven, and accompanied by similar songs, have also been recorded from the Yakut,[1] and the Yenisei Ostyak and the Yurak,[2] while ceremonies having much in common with these take place among the Buryat at the investiture of a new shaman.[3] There can, I think, be no doubt that the Tatar shaman is in full possession of all his faculties throughout the entire performance. Miss Lindgren notes the element of 'ritual drama' in the performances of Tungus shamans,[4] and Shirokogoroff also doubts the dissociation of the shamans.[5]

In this connection I must refer to an interesting observation made to me by Miss Lindgren in a personal communication. During the dance a Tungus shamaness wears a costume which can hardly have less than 40 lb. weight of iron attached,[6] largely in the form of iron pendants hanging free from the arms and the belt. The dance takes place within the constricted space between the fire and the members of the audience seated around the walls of the *yurt* (hut), and the shamaness's movements

---

1 See Sieroszewski, *Revue de l'Histoire des Religions*, vol. XVI (1902), pp. 331 f.
2 See Tretyakov, cited by Mikhailovski, *Journal of the Royal Anthropological Institute*, vol. XXIV, p. 67.
3 See Curtin, *A Journey in Southern Siberia* (London, 1909), p. 108; Czaplicka, *Aboriginal Siberia* (Oxford, 1914), p. 188.
4 See *Notes on the Reindeer Tungus of Manchuria*, published in *Abstracts approved for the Ph.D., M.Sc. and M.Litt. Degrees in the University of Cambridge*, 1935–6, p. 19 f. Cf. also Shirokogoroff, 'What is Shamanism?', *China Journal of Science and Arts* (1924).
5 *Loc. cit.*
6 E. J. Lindgren, 'Notes on the Reindeer Tungus of Manchuria', *Journal of the Royal Central Asian Society*, vol. XXII (1935), pp. 218 ff.; *Geografiska Annaler* (1935), p. 371.

during the dance appear abandoned and 'wild'. Yet although the pendants swing freely within an inch or two of the faces of the audience, during the performances which Miss Lindgren saw, the seeress never once struck any one during the dances. It is difficult to believe that such skill, acquired by long practice in a normal condition of mind, can have been mechanically applied by a virtual automaton in a condition of dissociation. Castagné also draws attention to the fact that during the ecstasy of the Kazak *baksha*, while he is flinging himself about with closed eyes, he can nevertheless lay his hands on anything he may happen to require.[1]

Among the peoples farther north in Siberia, who may perhaps be regarded as in a less advanced mental condition, we find the interesting phenomenon of shamans speaking *khorro*, 'shaman's language', during their fits of inspiration. *Khorro* is generally the language of a neighbouring people which the shaman does not himself understand. A Tungus shaman will sometimes speak, during his fit of inspiration, in Koryak, though he is said to be normally quite ignorant of the language.[2] Gmelin heard a Tungus shaman making a speech 'in a drawling chant', while the Tungus who were present chimed in. '*The language of the shaman's utterances was unknown.*'[3] The famous shaman Ilighin, of the vanished Kangienci tribe, who are said to have lived till the advent of the Russians on one of the eastern tributaries of the River Kolyma in north-eastern Siberia, is traditionally described as uttering

---

[1] Castagné, *Magie et Exorcisme chez les Kazak-Kirghizes et Autres Peuples Turks Orientaux* (Paris, 1930), p. 99.
[2] Recorded by Jochelson. See Czaplicka, *op. cit.* p. 231.
[3] See Mikhailovski, *op. cit.* p. 65.

incomprehensible words, 'speaking *khorro* (i.e. shaman) language', at the climax of his incantations.[1] This sometimes consists of a mixture of Koryak, Yakut, and Yukaghir.[2] These passages perhaps throw light on the statement made by Bogoras that although the Chukchee shaman sings tunes, his songs have no words, and there is no order in their succession.[3] There can be little doubt that these northern shamans are repeating a ritual which is not native to them. In an interesting passage, which is too long to quote, Kennan describes a form of nervous affection prevalent among the people of Anadirsk on the River Anadir near Behring Strait, especially among the women, which seems to consist of spasmodic outbreaks of second-sight, during which the patients talk 'languages which they have never heard, particularly Yakut'—a language said to be quite unknown to them in normal health.[4] It is possible that Kennan was actually listening to garbled accounts of the practice of private or family shamanism, which is said to be still widely prevalent among the tribes in North-Eastern Siberia. But the whole matter is closely paralleled by the practice of the lamas and Bön priests of Tibet, who in their incantations make use of corrupt Sanskrit formulae which they do not understand.[5]

This linguistic evidence can hardly be regarded as irrelevant to the question of the shaman's training, and

1 Shklovsky, *In Far North-East Siberia* (translated by Edwards, London, 1916), p. 157.
2 Czaplicka, *op. cit.* p. 231.
3 See *ib.* p. 230.
4 Kennan, *Tent Life in Siberia* (New York, 1910), pp. 343 ff.
5 Waddell, *Buddhism of Tibet*[2] (Cambridge: Heffer, 1934), p. 400; cf. also *ib.* p. 401, footnote 2; *Hastings' Encyclopaedia of Religion and Ethics*, s.v. *Tibet*.

the transmission of the intellectual side of the shamanistic tradition over wide areas. We have just seen that much of the poetry chanted by the Yakut and the Ostyak and Yurak shamans, as well as those of the Buryat, during their 'inspiration', bears a close resemblance to that of the Tatar shamans. This poetry is in its turn reminiscent of much of the plastic art of provincial Buddhism. These currents of artistic and intellectual culture can only be transmitted by intellectual means. It may be added that throughout northern Siberia the seer's inspiration is largely regulated, especially among the more mature, i.e. professional shamans, the methods of regulation being very similar to those of Europe.

Taking the Siberian evidence as a whole, it would seem probable that among the more advanced peoples of the south dissociation is no essential part of the shaman's condition, and is little in evidence here. Among the peoples farther north, who may be regarded according to civilised standards as less advanced, the evidence for dissociation appears to be stronger. I am not sure how far this may not be due to our greater ignorance of the languages and the oral poetry of these northern peoples. But it is said that even the *knout* of the Cossack has failed to arouse a Tatar shaman from his trance,[1] and there can be no doubt that even the Kazak *baksha* is able to acquire by a deliberate process a mental condition in which the body does not respond normally to external injury or shock, such as burning.[2] Among the more primitive

---

[1] Radlov, *Aus Siberien*, vol. II, p. 57.
[2] See, e.g., Shirokogoroff, *loc. cit.*; Lindgren, 'Reindeer Tungus o Manchuria', *Journal of the Royal Central Asian Society*, vol. XXII (1935), pp. 221 ff.

peoples of southern Asia the evidence for complete, or almost complete, trance is very strong. The Seligmans found the Vedda shamans going through an advanced performance resembling a charade or ballet, and chanting poems of considerable length as they worked themselves up to a condition of ecstasy; but in every instance actually recorded by the Seligmans the chanting seems to precede the ecstasy, and to cease when complete, or almost complete, dissociation supervenes.[1]

The Pacific is undoubtedly the richest area for the study of inspiration in every stage, from the Marquesan tohungas, the repositories of all the ancient chants and the composers of extempore ritual embodying the intellectual life and oral historical and genealogical records of this singularly intellectual people, to the Tongan children, who may, without preparation or warning, become 'possessed' by the god, and command the awestruck and attentive hearing of the chiefs. In the so-called *atuas* of the Marquesas,[2] and the female priestesses of Pele in Hawaii, we seem to get nearer to the root idea of inspiration than anywhere else; for here the claim is not for temporary possession, not for sporadic or regulated inspiration, but for permanent and actual divinity. 'I am Pele, and I shall never die.'[3] Some measure of discretion is, of course, necessary in regard to records made by early travellers in the Pacific as elsewhere—

[1] See C. G. and B. Z. Seligman, *The Veddas* (Cambridge, 1911), pp. 218 ff.
[2] C. S. Stewart, *A Visit to the South Seas*, vol. I (London, 1832), p. 244; F. W. Christian, *Journal of the Polynesian Society*, vol. IV, p. 202; cf. *ib.*, *Eastern Pacific Lands*, p. 167.
[3] Ellis, *Polynesian Researches*, vol. IV (London, 1831), p. 309 f.; C. S. Stewart, *op. cit.* vol. II, p. 100 f.

many of them untrained in critical methods; but in this case their independence and consistency is arresting. The words of the priestesses of Pele sound like faint echoes of the exalted human claims of the Mikados and the Celestial Dynasty; and they are undoubtedly to be connected with certain 'royal' strata of vocabulary formerly in use in Tahiti and the Marquesas, in which the ruling chief is spoken of in terms implying an aerial or celestial existence.[1]

Perhaps the most interesting evidence for the study of the relationship of poetic inspiration to manticism is afforded by the Island of Mangaia in the Cook Group. Here the priest of Motoro, who seems to have been a kind of royal chaplain as well as the high priest of the god of the royal line, practised prophetic frenzy when consulted,[2] and assumed at least a semblance of total dissociation, which is believed to have formed the model for the procedure of all other Mangaian priests of the tribal gods.[3] According to an ancient tradition, it was in virtue of their power of ecstasy that the priests of Motoro held office; and it is a strong testimony to the priests' belief in the genuineness of their own inspiration and absence of fake that when the 'king' insisted on having in office 'one who spoke from a foaming mouth',[4] no priest in Mangaia was found qualified, and a family of priests had

[1] Ellis, *op. cit.* vol. III, p. 113 f.; Christian, *op. cit.* pp. 162 f.
[2] Buck, *Mangaian Society* (Bernice P. Bishop Museum Memoirs, Bull. 122, 1934), p. 177. Cf. W. W. Gill, *Myths and Songs from the South Pacific* (London, 1876), pp. 19, 27.   [3] Buck, *loc. cit.*
[4] Whether we interpret this, with Gill, as speaking with *kava* still fresh on the lips, or whether the foaming mouth has reference to the 'possession', matters nothing. For *kava* was a drink of the priests and was partaken of in order to bring on a fit of frenzy or, as the Mangaians believed, possession by the god. See note 2, p. 23, below.

EVIDENCE OF MODERN ORAL LITERATURE 23

to be invited from Rarotonga to fill the office.¹ The ecstasy, it may be added, was deliberately regulated, like that of the Delphic Pythia, and was brought on by drinking an intoxicating drink and eating a special food.²

The close connection existing between divine inspiration and the art of poetry, which we have found to be so prominent a feature in the manticism of ancient Europe and of central and northern Asia, is made clear by these Mangaian *atuas*.³ It was customary in this island, and, indeed, in the entire group, to chant ritual dramatic poetry in honour of the gods Rongo and Tane, and of dead heroes who were sacrificed to them. These dramatic ritual chants were closely associated with the so-called *tapairu*, female spirits, or, as Gill translates the term, 'fairies',⁴ who are said to have come up through crevices in the earth to take part in the dances connected with them. The 'fairies', who were themselves closely associated with the god Tane, were in the habit of 'lodging' with the priestly dignitary whom Gill refers to as the 'Shore king', and who shared the hereditary rule of the island with the priest of Rongo, whom Gill calls the 'king of the Interior'; but the primary claims and functions of both these so-called 'kings' were priestly. It is interesting, therefore, that the ritual poetical dramas

1 Gill, *Myths*, pp. 19, 27.
2 Gill, *Myths*, p. 35; *Historical Sketches of Savage Life in Polynesia* (Wellington, 1880), p. 99.
3 For this term, see Gill, *Myths*, p. 35.
4 For references to the Mangaian 'fairies' see *ib.* pp. 256 ff. and *passim*; Buck, *op. cit.* p. 201; J. P. Andersen, *Myths and Legends of the Polynesians* (London, 1928), pp. 115 ff. For some discussion on the subject, and further references, the reader may refer to Chadwick, *Growth*, vol. III, pp. 293 ff. There can, in my opinion, be no doubt that these 'fairies' are the spirits of the dead.

referred to above were commonly performed near the dwelling of the 'Shore king' on the west side of the island, close to the statues of Rongo, and that they took place under definitely religious auspices.

Gill has recorded[1] extracts from a splendid series of the texts of these plays, which were mostly composed between the latter half of the seventeenth and the early years of the nineteenth century. It is important to note that for the greater part of this period the island was ruled by various members of the family of the 'inspired' priests of Motoro, who were also the 'temporal lords' of the island.[2] The majority of the ritual dramatic poetry of this period was composed either by the ruling priest himself, or by prominent members of his family. All these were notable poets. Under their régime and direct patronage and active composition the island produced one of the most remarkable schools of oral poetry which has ever been known. Many of these ritual dramas are definitely elegiac in character, and all are occasioned by death either from natural causes, or as a sacrifice to the gods. There is therefore a close analogy to the ritual elegiac and sacrificial poetry of the Siberian shamans, both in its origin among men given to prophetic frenzy, and also in the occasions for which it was composed. And here we may call attention in passing to the prominence of the drum in relation to Mangaian drama—both the great drum, known as the 'voice of Tane', which heralded

---

[1] Gill, *Myths*, *passim*.
[2] *Ib.* p. 36. They were known as the Ngati-Vara. They are said to have been the only tribe who managed to preserve their genealogies till the European period, when they were written down (Buck, *op. cit.* p. 57). The most famous member of their family was the great Mautara, priest of Motoro.

a religious and dramatic festival, and also to the smaller drum, associated with Tautiti, the son of Miru, ruler of the abode of the dead, which formed the musical accompaniment of the ritual dramas.

While the evidence for the mantic origin of this fine school of dramatic ritual poetry is especially rich in Mangaia, there is abundant evidence that ritual poetry with similar mantic associations was formerly widespread, if not universal, throughout the Pacific. In Hawaii a great body of *hula* poetry is associated with the Volcano goddess Pele and her family, with whom it is said to have originated, and whose priestess, as has been already mentioned, claimed identity with the goddess herself. In Tahiti ritual dramatic poetry connected with the life of the gods, and cosmogonic matters, and apparently resembling that of Mangaia in form, was enacted by a highly specialised guild, known as *arioi*, whose primary qualification for membership was evidence of divine inspiration, and whose headquarters were in the chief sanctuary of the Tahiti Group—the Island of Raiatea. Similar institutions appear to have flourished in the Marquesas, where the *kaulas*, as the priest-seers are called in this Group, were the principal composers. According to the traditional oral sagas of both the Marquesas and New Zealand, the art and poetic inspiration which shaped these ritual dramas, as well as all native learning, were derived from the land of departed spirits, and brought thence by a mortal, or a so-called 'fairy' man or woman, whose affinities seem to lie with the leader of the *arioi*. Everywhere throughout the Pacific the most ambitious and imaginative forms of poetical composition, as well as all intellectual matter, are directly derived through inspired seers or other persons endowed with divine ecstasy, from the spirit world.

Some light is thrown on the question as to how poetic inspiration came to be so closely connected with the mantic faculty by the oral literature of the Iban or Sea Dyaks of North Borneo, from whom we have a small but important body of oral mantic literature. From their lips dramatic poems have been recorded in which the gods are represented as visiting the earth at certain festivals, while the heroes of the past visit the Heavens to rescue the souls of mortals, and to make war on the gods, or alternatively to invite them to their feasts.[1] Among the most interesting of the Dyak dramatic ritual poems are the dirges and other poems recited by the seeresses[2] as a means of conducting the souls of the dead to their last resting-place.[3] In these chants various spirits are represented as passing to and fro as her emissaries between the world of mortals and the spirit world, while the seeress controls and regulates their actions, and herself conducts the souls of mortals to the land of the dead. Both in theme and treatment all these Dyak dramatic poems which tell of journeys to and fro between the land of mortals and the world of spirits bear a very close resemblance to the themes treated by the Tatar shamans,

---

[1] These poems have been recorded in English translation by the Ven. Archdeacon Perham in the *Journal of the Straits Branch of the Royal Asiatic Society*, nos. 2, 8, 10, etc. (1878–), and abridged versions have also been reprinted by Ling Roth in *The Natives of Sarawak and British North Borneo* (London, 1896).

[2] Mantic persons of the male sex are also common among the Sea Dyaks, but I have not seen any texts recorded from them. The word used of a seer is *manang*.

[3] Examples have been recorded, together with English translations, by the Rev. W. Howell, in the *Sarawak Museum Journal*, vol. 1 (1911).

to prose stories related in the eighth-century Japanese Chronicle known as the *Kojiki*, and to a large body of modern Polynesian oral saga, as well as to the narrative poetry and saga of Ladakh, Tibet and Mongolia.[1] It is, in fact, as we shall see, a favourite theme in the oral literature of a great arc on the periphery of eastern culture, with its centre in Buddhist Central Asia.[2] The task of marshalling and controlling the spirits, and of conducting the soul of the dead person to its last resting-place in the spirit world, is performed among the Sea Dyaks in dramatic poetry by a seeress, whose only mimetic act is her seat on a swing—possibly reminiscent of her spirit form, her power of flight. She neither acts nor dances, but in song rich in realistic detail she conducts her hearers for many hours through the long journey to the abode of the dead.

Everywhere, then, on the periphery of the great Eurasian continent, the peninsulas and outer islands, the steppes and tundras, which have preserved in written form or oral tradition the mantic habit and the traditions associated with it, we find the art of poetry in the closest association with the trance of the seer. We may go further, and say that it is the medium by which the seer links his fellow-men with the spirit world. Whether the seer journeys in his trance to the land of poetic inspiration, as in certain Polynesian traditions, or whether the god

---

[1] A. H. Francke, *Antiquities of Indian Tibet*, vol. I (Calcutta, 1914), p. 79; ib., 'Paladins of the Kesarsaga', *Journal and Proceedings of the Asiatic Society of Bengal*, vol. II, no. 10; vol. III, nos. 2, 5; J. J. Schmidt, *Die Talen Bogda-Gesser-Chans* (St Petersburg, 1839); David-Neel and Yongden, *The Superhuman Life of Gesar of Ling* (London, 1933).

[2] This does not necessarily mean that these themes originated in Buddhist thought.

takes possession of the medium and speaks through him, as at the sanctuary of Motoro in Mangaia, or whether the seer conducts his listeners to the divine presence by chanted poetry as among the Tatars, Yakut, Buryat and Dyaks, it is principally by means of his 'inspired' poetical utterances that his efficacy is gauged, both by himself, and by his audience.

The poetry of the seer appears to be rarely spoken, but most frequently chanted.[1] Indeed in Polynesia at least it may be said that chanted speech, if not actually metrical, is indistinguishable from poetry.[2] The artificial pitch and modulation of the voice are among the essential elements of Polynesian poetry. But what makes the exceptionally fine poetry of the Dyak seeress, what makes the high standard of mantic poetry elsewhere, is the intellectual effort of the seer. Whether the effort is made

[1] The importance in which music is held by mantic persons is aptly illustrated by the story of a famous *baksha*, as such persons are called among the Mohammedan Turks. Khorkoutt, who was regarded as the patron of all the *bakshas*, is said to have been at once a 'sorcerer, diviner, and musician', and to have taught his people the art of singing and of playing on the *kobuz*, the native stringed instrument of the Kazaks, while he himself was the originator of a particular form of 'epic' poetry. When he realised that his death was near, his first act was to make a new *kobuz* for himself, after which he divided his time between reciting prayers and verses from the Koran and singing to the accompaniment of his *kobuz*. After his death his *kobuz* was laid on his grave, and tradition asserts that for many years it played plaintive music every Friday in memory of its master (Castagné, *op. cit.* p. 61). Castagné also tells us (p. 67) that the *baksha* always carried with him a tambourine, a *domra* (a large instrument with some affinity to a banjo, but more elaborate), or a *kobuz*, and that all these are regarded as 'sacred'.

[2] It would be premature to make general statements on the essential constituents of Polynesian poetry as a whole, since the best Polynesian scholars have not reached any definite conclusions and are not always in agreement on the matter. For a brief discussion of the subject, see Chadwick, *Growth*, vol. III, pp. 239 ff.

consciously at the time, or mechanically by an automaton who, in a condition of dissociation later, merely works, involuntarily, virtually unconsciously, on traditional lines and at the mental level of his or her normal condition, is a matter about which all anthropologists anxiously await definite evidence.

In this problem it may be instructive to turn to African manticism, where the element of poetry is reduced to a minimum, and where the element of dissociation appears to be very fully developed. Here we seem to have a form of manticism the direct opposite to that of the Tatars, a form in which the spiritual is developed to the maximum, and the intellectual control appears to be reduced to a minimum. Yet even here we find that the ecstasy is commonly regulated, deliberately superinduced by stimulants and narcotics. Even here the ecstatic utterances, when chanted, are sometimes at least[1] in poetical form, and are found to be an elementary form of intellectual exercise. The few sentences recorded by Livingstone from the ecstatic utterances of an 'oracle' under the influence of *bang*, or Indian hemp, from the Makololo people on the Zambesi[2] resemble the Anglo-Saxon Gnomic verses in the Cottonian Collection.[3] The verses chanted by a seeress of a small tribe known as the Manganja, situated to the west of Lake Nyasa, seem also to refer to observations on the weather and wild animals.[4]

1 See, e.g., Grant, *A Walk across Africa* (London, 1864), p. 183; *Emin Pasha in Central Africa* (ed. Schweinfurth, London, 1888), p. 32.
2 *Narrative of an Expedition to the Zambesi and its Tributaries* (London, 1865), pp. 286 f.
3 See Chadwick, *Growth*, vol. I, p. 378.
4 Livingstone, *Last Journals of David Livingstone* ed. by H. Waller, vol. (London, 1874), p. 153 f.

The utterances of the seer Tlapone, from the Makololo on the Zambesi, give evidence of great political sagacity, though uttered in a fit of deliberately induced frenzy.[1] The observations of the prophets of the Zulu and neighbouring tribes recorded by early Europeans resident in South Africa bear witness to great political insight and intellectual curiosity.[2] The great Basuto chiefs, Moshesh and Mohlomi, were both intellectual men. Mohlomi in particular was a great seer, whose intellectual curiosity was insatiable, and whose personal researches in geography and political theory entitle him to recognition as a great field worker within the limits of native Basuto resources.[3]

Unfortunately it is only rarely that anyone thinks it worth while to record the utterances of these native seers. Observers are generally more concerned to give us the impression which the utterances of the seer make upon him than to record such utterances objectively. They are content to speak of 'random remarks', 'wild cries', 'ravings'. From exact notes such as those of Livingstone, Shooter, Ellenberger and some others we are able, however, to realise something of the interest of the native African seers in natural science, political theory, and moral problems. But even at best very little comes through to us of what passes in the mind of the seer; very few of the seers, encountered by accident, represent the best mantic intellects and spiritual visionaries of their people; and very few of those who have lingered on,

[1] Livingstone, *Missionary Travels and Researches in South Africa* (London, 1857), p. 86 f.
[2] Shooter, *Kafirs of Natal and the Zulu Country* (London, 1857), pp. 167 ff.
[3] See Ellenberger and McGregor, *History of the Basuto* (London, 1912), pp. 90 ff.

EVIDENCE OF MODERN ORAL LITERATURE 31

conservative remnants of fast vanishing schools of native thought, can give us a worthy idea of the best native thinkers of the civilisations which have vanished before Chaka's armies, and the white man's machinery.

Now if we compare these 'random remarks', 'ravings', etc., of the 'oracles' with the observations made by travellers on the system of education among the same people, it will be found that the former are closely related to the latter, and a natural outcome of it. Casalis tells us that as a part of the initiation ceremonies of the young Basuto, 'the scholars' are made to learn a number of little compositions, which generally consist in descriptions of animals or narrations of hunting and military expeditions.[1] These are embodied in poetical form. We are further told that the scholars employ themselves with the study of the principal phenomena of nature, such as the sun and moon, thunder, the earth, the rocks, the soil, rivers, and many other similar things.[2] Even historical information is given in songs to scholars at the initiation ceremonies.[3] The instruction is largely carried on in the form of question and answer,[4] and in this way we are able to understand the universal value attached to riddles and gnomes[5] as a means of oral education. The fact that in these African oral academies cosmogony is often substituted for science need cause no surprise. Early written literature—Norse, Greek, Sanskrit and Japanese—teems

1 Casalis, *The Basutos* (London, 1861), pp. 263 ff. For a similar form of learning among the Bantu tribes farther north see Stanley, *My Dark Companions and their Strange Stories* (London, 1893), p. 198 f.
2 Casalis, *op. cit.* p. 266.   3 Ellenberger and McGregor, *op. cit.* p. 14.
4 Casalis, *op. cit.* p. 265; Ellenberger and McGregor, *op. cit.* p. 297 f.
5 An excellent instance of the latter in native oral usage among the Baganda will be found in Stanley, *op. cit.* p. 270.

with the same form of learning. But the African is far ahead of any of our early written literatures as an expert field naturalist, and his observations of the habits of animals are generally more exact and scientific than our own, even when they are embodied in the form of fiction.

Among the southern Bantu our evidence for the intellectual side of manticism is perhaps fuller than in most parts of Africa. In Uganda, on the other hand, the case for total dissociation during 'inspiration' appears to me to be stronger than I have found elsewhere. Here poetry seems to be little developed, and manticism appears to a European observer to be at times wholly or almost wholly divorced from intellectual control or intellectual effort. Yet even here the casual observations of travellers such as Grant,[1] Emin Pasha,[2] Sir Samuel Baker,[3] and others, make it clear that minstrelsy and poetry are commonly accompanied by a certain degree of excitement, and are associated with the mantic class.

In Uganda official manticism has assumed an exceptionally interesting form. Here the traditional technique of the *mandwa* or medium consists of a perfect impersonation of the spirit by whom he or she is possessed. This means that the *mandwa* shall not only speak as the spirit, but actually reproduce the personality and the appearance of the spirit. The spirit which possesses the *mandwa* may be a dead person, and in this case the *mandwa* reproduces so far as possible in his own person, during his periods of possession, the appearance, bearing, voice and speech of the dead. The *mandwa* of a king who died

---

[1] *Op. cit.* p. 182 f.
[2] *Emin Pasha in Central Africa*, p. 32.
[3] *The Albert Nyanza*, vol. 1 (London, 1866), p. 391; cf. *ib.* p. 5.

centuries ago would speak in an obsolete dialect (see below). If the spirit is that of a god it may assume animal form, when the *mandwa*, during possession, imitates the movements and sounds of the animal. In many cases the possession of the temple *mandwa* was officially regulated, the frenzy being superinduced by drinking beer and smoking tobacco, after which he remained perfectly silent beside the temple fire.[1] Other methods were also used to induce frenzy.[2]

The *mandwas* of the zoomorphic deities were quite untrammelled in their technique. The *mandwa* of the python god Selwanga went down on his face and wriggled about like a snake, uttering peculiar noises and incomprehensible words.[3] The *mandwas* of certain rivers, worshipped under the form of a lion, roared like a lion when possessed.[4] The *mandwa* of the leopard god growled and rolled his eyes about like an angry beast when under the influence of the leopard ghost,[5] while the *mandwa* of the crocodile god worked his head about, opening his mouth and snapping it like a crocodile.[6] The wife of the *mandwa* on an island of the Sese Archipelago visited by Speke in Mutesa's company was evidently personating a frog.[7] A synod of heathen Baganda would have offered a historical pageant and a wild beast show unparalleled in the records of ecclesiastical art or practice.

Even inanimate objects and the forces of nature have their own *mandwa* who seek to symbolise by their movements and appearance the spirit by which they are

1 Roscoe, *Baganda*, p. 275 f.; cf. p. 312. 2 See *ib*. p. 313.
3 *Ib*. p. 322. 4 *Ib*. p. 318.
5 *Ib*. p. 335. 6 *Ib*. p. 336.
7 Speke, *Journal of the Discovery of the Source of the Nile* (Edinburgh, 1863), p. 395.

possessed. The *mandwa* of the earthquake god used to shake his body as if 'quaking',[1] while the *mandwa* of a river spirit wore a skirt hung about with shells which rippled as she walked. It is clear that throughout this system the technique employed by the *mandwa* is that of illusion. The appeal is not so much to the intellect as to the eye. The poetry of the seer, so highly developed among the Dyaks and the Polynesians, and even the Tatars, has disappeared. Its place is taken by mimesis. The spirit is made real to his worshippers by complete illusion. The supreme achievement of the Baganda church from a practical point of view is that it places the burden of imaginative effort not on the congregation but on the *mandwa*. It is somewhat as if the devil-dances of the popular ceremonies of the lamas of Tibet (e.g. at the New Year) were performed, not by large numbers and as a piece of ritual, but by individuals in a condition of total dissociation. The grip on the popular mind must have been correspondingly intense. It is not easy to grasp in a moment the profound religious thought which can have originated such a system, evolved its technique, and instituted it as a part of the politico-religious system throughout this highly developed country.

It is manifest both from an examination of their religious system and organisation, and from a careful reading of the history of the kings in their relations with the temple staffs, as this is given in the pages of Roscoe and of Kagwa, that the Baganda have nothing to learn from Europeans in the matter of religious speculation, religious organisation, and even religious propaganda.

[1] Sir Apolo Kagwa, *The Customs of the Baganda* (New York, 1934), p. 113 f.

EVIDENCE OF MODERN ORAL LITERATURE 35

It is especially on the official side, and in regard to institutions, that the achievement of Baganda religion has hardly received due credit in the pages of European books on the country. Their achievements in this direction can be gauged in some measure from a perusal of the works of the early missionaries, notably Felkin, Ashe and Roscoe. It is to be doubted if any annals show a church which has achieved a more complete command of the imagination among its own followers. When we learn that the Baganda prefer death to the loss of a limb, in order to enter upon the next life uncrippled:[1] and when we learn that in large numbers they have gone to execution cheerfully singing songs, assured of an immediate entrée to a continued existence, we realise that the effort of imagination has reached a perfect consummation. The spirit world is more real than the world of actuality. Could any priesthood achieve more?—for these cheerful condemned people are not the Latimers and Ridleys of Uganda, men set apart by a special calling for a life of religious thought, but the carpenters, gardeners, pages, and their fellows.

The most direct evidence which I have been fortunate enough to obtain on this subject myself was in some conversations which I had some years ago with the late Canon Roscoe. Two incidents were especially striking. The first, which is not directly connected with our subject, helps to throw light on the second. It relates to a woman who was acting at the time as Roscoe's gardener[2] in Entebbe, the capital of Uganda. Roscoe happened to ask her one day if she could tell him anything about a

1 Roscoe, *Baganda*, p. 281.
2 It was usual for such work to be done by the women.

certain king of Uganda[1] who had been dead for many generations—I think he said 200 or 300 years. 'O, yes,' replied the woman without a moment's hesitation, 'I'm his aunt.' Roscoe, naturally assuming that she had misunderstood him or made a mistake, hastened to explain more exactly which king he meant, and the period assigned to him by the unquestionable evidence of a comparison of the regnal lists. 'O, yes,' persisted the woman in a matter-of-fact way, 'I'm his aunt.' Roscoe, quite nonplussed, proceeded of course to question her at length, and it was in this way that he first came to make his researches into the remarkable clan system of inherited function and relationship. In short he discovered that his gardener happened to belong to the clan responsible for furnishing hereditary aunts to the hereditary supposititious court of the dead king,[2] and that she was, so-to-speak, in office.

The second incident related to me by Roscoe, which has a more direct bearing on our subject, relates to the so-called royal *mandwas* of Uganda. It is, of course, a well-known fact that in heathen times, that is to say until our own day, every king of Uganda had a *mandwa* appointed after his death to represent him, who was from time to time possessed by the spirit of the dead king. When the king's spirit came upon him, it was said that 'the king took him by the head'. The *mandwa* reproduced as far as possible the appearance and bearing, and even

---

[1] I think it was either Ndaula or Semakokiro.
[2] *The Customs of the Baganda*, p. 164, by Sir Apolo Kagwa, the *katikiro* or prime minister of Uganda. See also Roscoe, *Man*, vol. VII (1907), p. 161 f.; J. F. Cunningham, *Uganda and its Peoples* (London, 1905), p. 224 f.

the language of, the dead king. If I understand the system aright, when a *mandwa* died the spirit of the dead king descended upon another member of the same clan, who accordingly succeeded to the office.

When Roscoe was making enquiries for his researches into the past history of the country, he obtained his information from the best authorities he could find. These were chiefly the priests and *mandwas*, who were sent to him for the purpose by the *katikiro* or prime minister, Sir Apolo Kagwa. On one occasion, as one of these *mandwas* was sitting on the verandah relating to Roscoe the history of the kings, he suddenly began to talk absolutely unintelligibly. Roscoe tried to bring him to a more rational mood, but in vain—the unintelligible talk continued, till at last in some impatience Roscoe dismissed him from the verandah; but the man sank to the ground in the courtyard and continued to talk in the same vein. Roscoe went to the *katikiro* and asked him why he had sent such a useless person to him. In great surprise the *katikiro* asked him to explain, but when Roscoe told him what had happened the *katikiro* said in impressive and awe-struck tones: 'How I wish I had been there! The king had him by the head.'[1] The spirit of the dead king had come upon him, and the man, we were assured by Roscoe, was talking in the obsolete form of *Luganda* spoken in the lifetime of the dead king three centuries ago.[2]

---

[1] This is the phrase current in *Luganda* for supernatural possession.
[2] The *mandwa*, or 'medium', of the gods also 'speaks in tones not his own, using many obsolete words, so that it is difficult even for his brother priests to understand what he says': Roscoe, *Man*, vol. VII (1907), p. 163. Cf. also Kagwa, 'The so-called gods were formerly human beings. Their attendants imitated their voices and claimed to be inspired by them': *op. cit.* p. 124.

Roscoe himself regarded this as astonishing, and it was clear to both my companion and myself as we listened that he had no explanation to offer. The suddenness of the ecstasy, and its apparent inopportuneness, and the fact of the man speaking in a language no longer known or understood seemed like a clear case of total and unregulated dissociation, indeed of true possession by the dead. It was not till long afterwards that a more detailed study of the temple and clan systems of Uganda suggested to me a possible explanation on simple and rational lines. Now we know that in Uganda each clan responsible for providing the *mandwas* of each of the dead kings had to transmit orally and mimetically the characteristics of the dead king at the time of his decease. Thus the *mandwa* of King Kigala who died at a very advanced age used to behave as if he were old, though actually he was quite young when Roscoe knew him. He would limp, slaver at the mouth, wear the expression of an old man.[1] The *mandwa* of the god in the Sese Archipelago assumed a similar demeanour during Speke's visit.[2] I have no doubt that in the clan to whom Roscoe's *mandwa* belonged the obsolete dialect was preserved— how much of it we do not know—as a part of the mantic technique, as the *mandwas* of the gods make use of obsolete words and phrases (see above), and as we have seen some of the shamans of northern Siberia speak languages which they do not understand.

It is, of course, quite possible that the ecstasy came on the *mandwa* of Uganda unawares, but the evidence is capable of a different interpretation. It may be that the

[1] Roscoe, *Baganda*, p. 216 f.; and in a personal communication to me.
[2] Speke, *op. cit.* p. 395.

occasion which seemed to Roscoe so ill-timed for a mantic display struck the *mandwa* as quite the most suitable. When asked to tell Roscoe what he knew of past kings, is it unnatural that he should take, either deliberately or involuntarily, through force of mental habit, the most obvious means at his disposal to recreate that particular portion of the past to which he alone had the entrée? It may be that the concentration of his thoughts on a certain reign was the prescribed technique by which, as *mandwa*, he was accustomed to prepare himself for his fit of 'possession', his mantic demonstration. We do not know. It is a part of the value of mantic studies that they bring home to us constantly how traditional are our own thought sequences, and how alien from the spheres of thought of the peoples whom we are studying.

It will be seen that in general the evidence from modern peoples in Asia and Polynesia corresponds closely with that of ancient Europe. Here also we find the same close association between poetry and the inspired utterance of the seer; the same lofty status accorded to those who can compose and chant poetry which will put man into communion with the spirit world and reveal to him the things which are past, and present, and to come. Here also we find that the gift of inspiration receives high official recognition, and is accordingly subject in some measure to regulation. Perhaps it is not too much to say that the prophet is the most important person in the community. In other words, the communion between man and the spirit world is still of paramount importance, and inspiration a living reality.

In Africa the gift of poetry and the intellectual side of prophecy are less highly developed, though their close association is still maintained. In Africa, however, the spiritual aspect is even more prominent than in Asia and Polynesia, and here we find it even forming a fundamental element in the kingship. The temporal ruler must be qualified by divine communion and divine inspiration, and he himself has the power to inspire his future mediums. The spirit of the divine king does not die, or even pass from this world. Ritually, by permanent institutions, the past is kept alive, the dead go on living. The celebration of the dead in dramatic form, which we have seen to take place seasonally, and at great festivals in Polynesia and ancient Japan, is a permanent institution in parts of Africa. It would seem probable that in such permanent re-enactments of the past as we find in Africa we have the birth of drama.

On the whole the evidence suggests that African manticism represents an earlier phase of manticism than that of Eurasia and Polynesia. In Africa the appeal is to the eye rather than to the ear. The permanent and continuous re-enactment of the past as against the seasonal drama of Polynesia suggests that spiritual life is held in even higher esteem here, and plays an even greater part in the political and economic life. In accordance with this also the evidence suggests that complete dissociation is a more recognised form of official manticism here than in Eurasia or Polynesia. But intimate detail about African prophetic inspiration must still be awaited from African specialists before any final pronouncement can be made. In this respect we await with the greatest interest what the educated African alone can tell us in the future.

CHAPTER III

INSPIRATION: THE SEER'S CALL, AND HIS ARTISTIC AND SPIRITUAL GIFTS

THE results of our survey so far enable us to make certain general inferences. Among the peoples of ancient Europe, and in primitive and backward communities of the present day everywhere inspiration refers not only to the gift of song, and of polished and persuasive speech in general, but also to the subject-matter. The association of inspiration and knowledge of whatever kind acquired by supernatural means is ancient and widespread. Inspiration, in fact, relates to revealed knowledge. Revelation covers the whole field of human consciousness. It includes knowledge of the past and the hidden present, as well as the future. Revelation of the future is generally less important than is commonly supposed. Among backward peoples perhaps knowledge of the present plays the most important part, especially of the hidden present. Miss Lindgren heard a Tungus shamaness shamanise in order to learn, among other things, whether a Cossack trader, imprisoned by the Chinese, was still alive[1]—an example of knowledge of the hidden present on private matters acquired by inspiration. The oracular responses of the Delphic oracle, recorded in poetical form by the priests, are usually examples of the hidden present acquired by inspiration, and these often concern political matters. But the knowledge displayed by inspiration on

[1] *Journal of the Royal Central Asian Society*, vol. XXII (1935), pp. 221 ff.

political matters need not necessarily be occult. It may merely show exceptional discernment. The great *wanana*,[1] or political 'inspired poems' (the word is usually translated 'prophecy'), on current politics composed and recited by the Hawaiian official seers are examples of the latter. They are sustained and highly elaborate artistic productions sometimes extending over several hundred lines. The 'inspired' element in these *wanana* is, it may be safely assumed, merely a conventional literary motif.

Inspiration relating to matters of the past includes historical and genealogical traditions and speculations, and antiquarianism. But all matters of science and knowledge generally, as well as moral and didactic matter, may be learnt by inspiration. In early Thrace we have seen that the seers were deeply interested in natural philosophy and theology, as well as in other scientific matters. In these features they have much in common with the mantic classes of ancient Gaul, as well as with the seers and poets of ancient Ireland. Their affinities with the Brahmins, the learned seers of the Sanskrit literature of ancient India, are equally striking. Thracian mantic thought, as we have seen, appears to offer a link between these different regions.

Such knowledge, being acquired in part by a private process, is partly of a subjective character. In so far as this is so it differs from scientific knowledge, born of the classical world of thought. The ancient Irish, who were familiar with both types of knowledge, appear to have distinguished *sous* and *fius*, or Latin 'overt', 'scientific', objective, learning in the broader sense, from *imbas*, or

[1] *Fornander Collection of Hawaiian Antiquities*, Third Series, vol. VI (Honolulu, 1919–20), pp. 368 ff.

HIS ARTISTIC AND SPIRITUAL GIFTS 43

'occult' knowledge, 'revealed' to the seer by inspiration. The Irish *filid* in the later stages of their history were experts in both types of knowledge, so far as their opportunities and environment permitted. Linguistic and historical evidence point strongly to this being the case also among the *bakshas* of the western Turks and the shamans of the eastern Turks and other Siberian peoples.[1] It is the same distinction as that between the testimony to God as seen in Amos's vision while shepherding his flocks, and that in the expression used by St Luke at the opening of his Gospel: 'having traced the course of all things accurately from the first', i.e. with due objective scrutiny and research, which implies a use of criticism by impersonal standards for the apprehension of truth seen objectively. In studying the traditional learning of more backward peoples, however, the chief difficulty is to understand the true nature and limits of knowledge acquired by *imbas*. There are undoubtedly in Africa many methods of handing on exact knowledge of the past, as well as of acquiring exact information about the present, which are either wholly unsuspected, or woefully misunderstood by ourselves when we happen to be ignorant of the traditional methods of native thought and of native education. When the late *katikiro* of Uganda tells us that traditional history was transmitted orally by means of a series of pegs, each named after a historical personage, such as the kings, their wives, chiefs, etc., and that children were trained from childhood to name each peg and to memorise the traditions associated with the persons so named,[2] we feel ourselves on familiar

[1] See, e.g., Castagné, *op. cit.* pp. 59 ff.
[2] Kagwa, *op. cit.* p. 78.

ground; but the temples of the Baganda kings, with their hereditary courts and *mandwas* keeping the past alive by a perpetual re-enactment, constitute a form of historical document which we are ill-equipped to decipher.

Our ignorance of the languages of many seers, and of most mantic classes of our own day, has tended to obscure the importance of the intellectual aspect of the seer's functions. But where seers are an important and honoured class, and where their language is understood, the seer's intellectual achievements are always recognised and emphasised in their own communities. The *Brahmins*, or rather *rishis*, of ancient India, the mantic classes of ancient Gaul, and the *filid* of ancient Ireland were always recognised to be the most intellectual classes in the community. It is actually so among modern peoples. We have seen that the Polynesian seers are responsible for the native oral learning of the Pacific, with its great wealth of historical tradition.[1] The Siberian shamans are said to be reliable transmitters of ancient traditions.[2] According to the Buryat scholar Sandschejew, who was himself brought up to be a shaman in early life, the shamans are responsible for the preservation and transmission of all their aesthetic-poetical riches 'which are represented by their vast epics, poems, hymns, and songs'.[3] In Uganda Roscoe found the priests and *mandwas* the best and most

[1] It would be idle to give references, which could easily amount to many hundreds. But I would call special attention to the publication by S. Percy Smith, *The Lore of the Whare Wananga*, 2 vols., published in *Memoirs of the Polynesian Society*, vols. III, IV (New Plymouth, 1913, 1915), in which the traditional oral learning, both exoteric and esoteric, of certain tribes, is recorded from the recital of old Maori *tohungas*, or native scholars of oral learning.
[2] K. Donner, *Sibirien* (Helsingfors, 1933), p. 232.
[3] *Anthropos* (1927), p. 306.

HIS ARTISTIC AND SPIRITUAL GIFTS 45

reliable sources of information for the past history of the country.[1]

The process by which the knowledge which has been revealed to the seer is transmitted to his fellow-men is known as 'prophecy', i.e. inspired speech. Wherever poetry, as we understand the term, is a highly cultivated art, prophetic utterance is couched in poetical form, and where the art of writing is unknown it is accompanied by music in some form. This connection is clearly very ancient. The Greek word ὀμφή for the oracular voice of a deity is identical with our word *song*. The use of music is undoubtedly due partly to the practical necessity of couching prophecy in the most impressive and far-reaching vehicle of expression, partly to a desire to reach the spirits, who are assumed to be far away, and to 'publish' orally in the most impressive form. But it is also ritual in purpose, for music is the language of spirits, and the principal means of communication between the spirits and humanity.[2] Where poetry, as we understand the term, does not exist, other artificial modes of expression are used, as we have seen. The artistic and literary element in the seer's performance is of great importance if he is to impress and 'carry' his audience.

The aesthetic aspect of the seer's art is as carefully cultivated as the intellectual. Among the Tatars the shamans have developed an ambitious artistic creation in which extempore poetry and song are combined with mimesis and the dance to form an elaborate form of ritual ballet, in which the shaman is at once the author and the

---

[1] *Baganda*, p. x; cf. also Kagwa, *op. cit.* p. 164.
[2] I have written more fully on this subject elsewhere; see *Journal of the Royal Anthropological Institute*, vol. LXVI (1937), pp 297 ff.

sole performer.[1] In Uganda, before the conversion of the country, the mediums practised a form of mimesis which, as we have seen, was masterly in its way. In Polynesia the mantic recitals are no less elaborate, but here, as always in Polynesia, the intellectual endeavour has been to achieve literary excellence rather than illusion, whether of action or of scene. The picturesque and telling imagery, and the splendid rhetoric of the Hawaiian *wanana* or 'inspired poems', and the beauty of the Mangaian ritual chants have been already referred to, though it would be impossible here to do justice to their artistic concentration and the relevance of theme and allusion throughout these fragile and exquisite compositions, intended to be recited and forgotten. In the poems in which the seeress of the Sea Dyaks conducts the soul to the land of the dead, we follow her as in her song she plies her little canoe down the winding reaches of the great Borneo river, past vast forests, through dangerous rapids, along the settlements

[1] Except for the *bash tutkan kiski*, the assistant who takes part in the whole ceremony as the shaman's assistant. The part played by 'assistants', their exact functions, and their relationship to apprentices, is one which needs investigating. Miss Lindgren has several times spoken to me of a certain Tungus of her acquaintance, belonging to the Dagur, who, though making no claim to be a shaman himself, had a great 'flair' for shamans, and never missed a ceremony if he could help it. He would walk many miles to be present, and seems to have acted as a kind of assistant and master of ceremonies. In Miss Lindgren's private film he is present during the ceremony performed by a shamaness, to whom he and another shaman are acting in the capacity of assistants. Is his function in any way traditional? Is he serving any kind of apprenticeship? Does he aspire ultimately to the function known among the Yakut as that of the 'little shaman'? It is noteworthy that Castagné speaks of two assistants of the Kazak *bakshas*, while the Buryat and Yakut shaman generally had a greater number, sometimes as many as nine. Miss Fegan tells me in a personal communication that the Court Jester of the Emir of Katsina on the River Niger generally has two little boys, his 'apprentices', in attendance on him.

HIS ARTISTIC AND SPIRITUAL GIFTS 47

on the banks. We watch the occupations of the various groups of inhabitants, holding parley before we are allowed to pass on. The functional importance of the seeress's aesthetic gifts is made clear by her closing words, in which she claims that by her singing the dead are comfortably lodged in Hades:

My voice has been heard at the landing-place...
The sweetness of my voice has travelled gracefully...
And has echoed on the...staircase of the people of Hades...
The utterance of my tongue has lodged up in the long straight house;
After my continual calling all have come in and are seated in a row.[1]

The aesthetic value of the seer's art is not lost on the audience. Radlov tells us that when an Altai shaman is reciting not a sound escapes from his audience; their pipes go out, their eyes are riveted on the shaman, and for a long time after he has ceased to speak no one moves. All are spell-bound. Radlov himself was spell-bound.[2] Stadling mentions that the Chukchee cover many miles to hear a good shaman singer.[3] The Dyaks listen with rapt attention to their seeress, whose performance takes many hours, sometimes all night.[4] There has already been a movement in the Buryat press for enrolling the shaman, with his dramatic talent and his gift of improvisation, in the State Theatre.[5]

1 Howell, *loc. cit.*
2 *Aus Sibirien*, vol. I, p. 55.
3 *Shamanismen i Norra Asien* (Stockholm, 1912), pp. 130 ff. Stadling lays great emphasis on the importance of the aesthetic and artistic side of shamanism throughout Siberia.
4 Howell, *loc. cit.*
5 Sandschejew, 'Welt-Anschauung und Schamanismus der Alaren-Burjaten,' *Anthropos*, 1927, p. 306.

48 INSPIRATION: THE SEER'S CALL

In the absence of organisation, the high standard of the intellectual and aesthetic gifts of the seer are fostered by a competitive spirit which is bound to have a beneficial effect on his art. We read constantly of contests between sages. When a new shaman is needed in a Tungus tribe, the choice is sometimes made by a 'special examination, made by the seniors of the tribe, of a number of rival claimants in order to find out which of the candidates can shamanise'.[1] We are reminded of the story of Calchas and Mopsos, and of the rival sages in Sanskrit literature and in Tatar oral poetry. Early Norse and Irish records also offer many instances. In all these, general knowledge, especially knowledge of natural—or unnatural natural—history, and of the physical Universe plays a large part. Great prominence is usually given to poetic diction and skill in the pedantic use of phrase and artificial language (rhetoric). Always skill in language is stressed.

These competitions of wit and wisdom and skill in poetry often take the form of riddle contests, which may be said to be universal in oral, as in written literature. We have seen (p. 31 above) that these are a favourite device for the education of the young among the Basuto. Among the Russian peasants,[2] as well as in Ladakh,[3] they form part of the marriage negotiations—intelligence tests to ascertain the cultural qualifications of bride and bridegroom. Riddle competitions are popular also among the Kazak and the Yakut.[4] In Polynesia contests between

1 Shirokogoroff, *loc. cit.*
2 See Ralston, *Songs of the Russian People*[2] (London, 1872), p. 348; Chadwick, *Growth*, vol. II, p. 211.
3 Francke, *Tibetische Hochzeitslieder* (Hagen und Darmstadt, 1923).
4 Vambéry, *Türkenvolk* (Leipzig, 1885), p. 295.

HIS ARTISTIC AND SPIRITUAL GIFTS 49

tohungas take a similar form, while the oral literature of the Tatars, and the written literatures of ancient India, Ireland, and the North offer innumerable instances of this form of competition between rival sages.[1] We may refer in particular to the Riddle Contest between the royal sage Heithrekr and the disguised god Othin in the Norse *Hervarar Saga*, ch. x.[2]

This competitive element, combined with the absence of central organisation, and the insistence of the seer on the divine origin of his inspiration, has undoubtedly been of enormous importance in the history of poetry. The seer must command a hearing, not by virtue of his office (for he can hardly be said to hold one), but by virtue of his ability to convince both himself and his fellows of his superior gifts—spiritual, intellectual, artistic. Competition stimulates effort, public opinion raises the standard, and the absence of a written text keeps effort ever fresh, and the art dynamic. We may refer again (cf. p. 23 above) to the fine ritual dramatic poetry of the Island of Mangaia in Central Polynesia, composed and stimulated by a dynasty of seers. This poetry is a lasting testimony to the healthy and valuable results of poetic inspiration. The priestly rulers of Mangaia, who ruled from the latter half of the seventeenth till the early part of the nineteenth century, transformed the island from a scene of endless guerrilla warfare into a school of poetry unique in the history of oral literature. But the mantic art has been equally associated with the gift of poetry throughout the

---

[1] Shklovsky, *op. cit.* p. 46.
[2] Translated by N. Kershaw, *Stories and Ballads of the Far Past* (Cambridge, 1921), pp. 113 f. References to all these will be found in Chadwick, *Growth*, vols. II and III.

50 INSPIRATION: THE SEER'S CALL

Pacific. The dramatic poetry of the *arioi* of Tahiti (cf. p. 25 above) was composed and recited by a guild, whose first qualification for membership was the ability to prove divine inspiration by falling into ecstasy.

The inspiration of the seer is derived from a variety of sources. It may be like Hesiod's from supernatural beings; or like that of northern seers from an inherent power within themselves; or like that of Cormac MacAirt, the High-king of Ireland, who is traditionally believed to have flourished in the third century, from a supernatural region which he visited in an ecstasy. Irish, Welsh, and Norse traditions know of inspiration received in a vision during battle, like that of Merlin in Cumberland, and Suibhne Geilt in Ireland, who both became great mantic poets, according to tradition. People so inspired are said in Irish and Norse to be *geilt*. The dead are among the commonest sources of inspiration. It may be preserved human heads, like the head of Mimir, which is said to have told the Norse god Othin 'many hidden things'. The belief that the call to manticism is received from a dead ancestor is very common.

A very large amount of information is available on this subject from modern peoples, but it is so astonishingly varied that it is not always easy to see where the common elements lie. A Zulu prophet will without warning suddenly rush from home and seek solitude and asceticism, to return later, fearfully emaciated, his neck wreathed in snakes, and with the gift of 'prophecy' fully developed.[1] The great Basuto prophet Mohlomi received his call in youth by imagining that the roof of his hut opened above

[1] See Shooter, *op. cit.* p. 191.

HIS ARTISTIC AND SPIRITUAL GIFTS

him, and he himself was raised to the sky where a great multitude of people were assembled.[1]

Among the Buryat shamanism seems to come upon a person commonly as the result of a vision. Sandschejew relates[2] the tradition of a vision which appeared to the white shaman, Ungin Shaman Ucha, who lived *c.* 180 years ago, and whose descendant in the eighth generation on the mother's side is Sandschejew himself, the writer of the article, who was himself instructed in youth by the shamans to become one of themselves. The vision deprived his ancestor for the time being of all power of movement. For some time the young man felt himself unwell, and eventually he presented himself before the shamans, telling them that two riders on fox-red horses had appeared to him, riding from north to south. The shamans revealed to him that he had received the shamanistic 'call' (*ucha*) from the chief of the Heavenly rulers; and from that time he became a famous shaman. The same writer also narrates a story of the 'call' of a shamaness, which he recorded from a shamaness named Schagai. The story relates that an eagle appeared to a shepherdess on successive occasions and stole her lambs. 'Then the maiden came to the conclusion that it was not an eagle which came flying to her but the spirit of her ancestor, and that on this account she would be compelled to be a shamaness.'[3]

In most countries the transports of the seer are artificially regulated. This is natural where ecstasy is an old-established institution, and held in high esteem. The

[1] Ellenberger and McGregor, *op. cit.* p. 90.
[2] *Anthropos* (1927), p. 943.
[3] *Ib.* p. 305.

mantic vision is often superinduced, as we shall see, by the employment of a definite discipline both physical and mental, and is reduced or elaborated to a definite technique. The gift of manticism can be acquired, and the technique, to a large extent, is a matter of practice. The areas in the Old World where manticism is very fully developed in modern times, e.g. Siberia, Uganda, Mangaia, show this most clearly. Taking the evidence as a whole, it does not appear that it is the gift of inspiration which is inherited,[1] but rather the tendency to a contemplative life; or perhaps even this is only acquired by a growing child as a habit of thought from his elders, or his environment. The tendency is neither racial nor confined to any area. It appears to be most fully developed in communities where change comes slowly and late, and where the history of thought does not move in a rapid series of revolutions.

Unfortunately our evidence—whether from ancient records or modern observation—is less extensive than we could wish in regard to the seer's special training for his office; but some outstanding facts may be gleaned from such material as is available. Chief of these is the importance of segregation and of instruction. It is true that Hildén tells us[2] that among the Altai Tatars no training is given; but we find it difficult to accept this. Among the Khingan Tungus some of the best shamans and shamanesses undergo a thorough training from an

---

[1] We are, of course, frequently told that among certain peoples and tribes 'the shaman call is inherited'; see, e.g., K. Hildén, 'Om Shamanismen i Altai', *Terra, Geografiska Föreningens Tidskrift*, vol. xxviii (1916), p. 132. See also Castagné, *op. cit.* p. 59.
[2] Hildén, *loc. cit.*

HIS ARTISTIC AND SPIRITUAL GIFTS 53

old shaman.¹ This is common elsewhere also. According to Niemojowski² children consecrated for the office of shaman are taught by old men, doubtless shamans themselves, not only the outward form and ceremonies, but the medical properties of plants and herbs, with the different ways of forecasting the weather by the behaviour and migrations of animals. Castagné also mentions that among the Kazak-Kirghiz children are often set apart at an early age to be trained as *bakshas*, as seers are called among these people.³

In Polynesia it is clear that both the professional seer and certain aristocratic and ruling chiefs with mantic functions underwent a special training from early childhood. The last high priest of the Island of Rarotonga in the Cook Group told the late scholar S. P. Smith that he was sent as a child to live in seclusion in a cave with his mother, and here he was taught by his father the historical traditions and genealogies of his island.⁴ Sagas of early mantic heroes, such as Maui⁵ and Kura⁶—the latter recorded from Tahiti, the Marquesas, and other islands of the Central Pacific—ascribe to them a curiously similar mode of training. The heir to the throne in Mangareva in the Gambier Islands is said to have been

---

1 See Lindgren, *Journal of the Royal Central Asian Society*. Further references are cited in my paper 'Shamanism among the Tatars of central Asia', in the *Journal of the Royal Anthropological Institute*, vol. LXVI (1936), pp. 75 ff.
2 *Siberian Pictures*, vol. I (London, 1883), p. 13.
3 Castagné, *op. cit.* p. 59.
4 *Journal of the Polynesian Society*, vol. VIII, p. 61.
5 See the Rarotongan version referred to by S. P. Smith, *Journal of the Polynesian Society*, vol. IV, p. 256; *Hawaiki*⁴ (Wellington, 1921), p. 156.
6 Smith, *Hawaiki*,⁴ p. 156. Fuller references are given in Chadwick *Growth*, vol. III, part II.

secluded in childhood for six or seven years on a mountain top, in the company of certain women.[1] At the age of ten he was circumcised and tattooed and instructed in his ancestral history.[2] A similar custom prevailed in Mangareva.[3] It is clear that reflection in solitude, and instruction, formed the chief elements in the early life of mantic persons in Central Polynesia.[4]

On this subject probably our richest source of information is to be found in Celtic tradition, both Irish and Welsh. The evidence is too extensive and too complex to be considered here in any detail. But the traditions of the childhood and upbringing of such seers as Amargin, Finn, Corc, or Morann from Ireland, and of Taliesin from Wales, have certain features in common, both with one another and with the Polynesian evidence. The chief of these are the importance of a period of solitude and segregation in youth, and the instruction given by an older mantic person.[5] In general also the feminine companionship for the youthful seer is stressed here also. At a later stage in the seer's preparation it would seem that in Celtic tradition the seer's mantic and his poetic inspiration are alike derived from a woman, whether a sister, or a supernatural being. The Norse god Othin

---

[1] S. P. Smith, *Journal of the Polynesian Society*, vol. XXVII, pp. 120 f.
[2] Caillot, *Mythes, Légendes et Traditions des Polynésiens* (Paris, 1914), p. 150.
[3] Dumont d'Urville, *Voyage au Pôle Sud et dans l'Océanie* (Paris, 1841, etc.), vol. II, part I, p. 428.
[4] It is not confined to the Central groups, however, but is found also in Hawaii. See J. P. Andersen, *Myths and Legends of the Polynesians*, p. 302.
[5] The evidence is plentiful and clear enough in Irish tradition. In Wales it is not so obvious, chiefly owing to the fact that the stories have reached us in a much later form; but a close comparison and critical examination of even the Welsh stories in the light of the Irish traditions demonstrates their essential agreement in the matters stated above.

HIS ARTISTIC AND SPIRITUAL GIFTS 55

derived his mantic and poetic inspiration from a spring or cauldron guarded by women. The erotic character traditionally ascribed to the Sanskrit seers may be seen from a number of the stories related of them in the *Mahabharata*.

Perhaps the most universal aspect of manticism is the derivation of inspiration and the gift of poetry from the dead. The evidence is too extensive to be treated here, but we shall see in a later chapter that the visits of mantic persons to the land of the dead—whether in the form of narrative or of ritual—are found in very similar form in the literature of the ancient Assyrians, the Greeks, the Japanese Chronicle composed in the early eighth century, in early Norse, and in the modern oral sagas and poetry of the Tibetans, Mongols, the Tatars, the Yakut, Tungus, Polynesians, and Sea Dyaks. We have seen that a preserved human head is the chief mantic property of the god Othin. But the closest and most interesting instance of this connection between manticism and the dead is the institution in Uganda which in the past supplied a royal medium to every dead king, who from time to time became possessed by the spirit of the dead king, and impersonated him in public. The connection with drama is here very close, as we have seen. Can the *No* plays of Japan, all of which appear to be ghost plays, have had some such origin?

But manticism is also very widely associated with birth, and with rebirth. In Sanskrit literature the Brahmins figure largely as the givers of children, especially to childless kings. In Tatar oral poetry, especially the poems recorded from the Abakan Steppe and neighbouring regions on the Yenisei, one of the commonest themes is that of a supernatural old man, who is in reality God, who appears suddenly to a childless couple, and, having granted their request that they may have a child, disappears as suddenly as he has come. In early Norse legendary sagas, and in the poems of the Edda, we have an extensive literature relating to the cult of the land of rebirth, which is also represented as a land of music and of song. This is the home not only of the early legendary king Guthmundr, whose followers 'do not die, but live for many generations',[1] but also of Othin, the god of battle and bloodshed and violent death, and the origin and giver of the art of poetry. The learned Danish historian, Saxo Grammaticus, who flourished about 1200, and whose work is a great storehouse of early northern tradition, affords us many traces of the same association of ideas. In early Irish literature the lands visited by mantic persons during ecstasy, especially the form of ecstasy known as *baile*, is a land in which the descendants of the mantic person are categorically enumerated in prophetic form by a seer or a god who prophesies in the form of chanted poetry as a result of drinking from a cauldron of inspiration. The mantic classes of ancient Gaul 'proclaimed souls to be immortal',[2] and taught that after death the souls of men were reborn.[3] There can be little doubt that it is largely the seer's promise of immortality in one form or another which has given him such a great and lasting hold on men's homage in Europe, Asia, Polynesia, and Africa. In Africa, indeed, rebirth is made a living reality in the person of the

1 *Hervarar Saga*, ch. 1 (translated by Kershaw, *op. cit.* pp. 87 ff.).
2 Ammianus Marcellinus, xv, ix, 8.
3 Diodorus Siculus, v, xxviii, 6.

mandwa, in whose person the spirit of the dead lives on. The African *mandwa*, alone among seers, has succeeded where Gilgamesh failed. He gives to men the gift of immortality in a concrete and tangible form.

It is this function of the seer as a messenger between the spirit and the material world which gives him his highest claim to the reverence of his society. He alone can convoy the spirit of the dead to the living, and he alone can convoy the living in safety to their last abode among the dead. He alone can bring knowledge from the gods and from the spirits of the underworld. He alone can interpret the spiritual messages which he receives to his fellow-men and present them in a form which will carry enlightenment and conviction.

To this end he trains himself by a rigorous spiritual discipline. By his early segregation, and by his devotion to a contemplative life, by his periods of concentration in seclusion he trains himself as a spiritual and intellectual specialist. Owing to the absence of print and publication he is dependent on the immediate effect of his spoken word and such additional appeal as music, dance and dramatic presentation can add to his poetical utterance. Competition and publicity are his stimulus, and the measure of his success. On the whole it may be safely said that the inspired prophet and seer is the leading intellectual and artistic influence in primitive and backward society.

CHAPTER IV

THE MANTIC TECHNIQUE AND THE ARTIFICIAL REGULATION OF ECSTASY

THE means employed in the regulation of ecstasy are many and various. In ancient Europe and in Asia the seer's ecstasy is stimulated by various artificial means, such as special food, generally vegetarian, special drink, generally intoxicating, or at least stimulating, narcotic or stimulating fumes. The importance attached by the seer to the stimulating drink is illustrated by the *kava* drink of the Mangaian priests (cf. p. 22 above), and by the *soma* plant of Sanskrit poetry, which is personified as 'lord of speech', and as a poet, seer, and sage. *Soma* even has the power of granting immortality.

Other properties play a part in the regulation of manticism, such as the professional costume, the staff, and the musical instrument. These are widespread throughout Europe and Asia. The cloak of the Irish poets and seers, largely composed of birds' feathers, recalls the costumes of the Siberian shamans, which are most commonly in the representation of some bird or, less commonly, some animal.[1] The costume of the Norse seeress in *Thorfinns Saga*, like that of the god Othin, forms a regular shaman's outfit, with its high peaked hat, cloak, high boots, and gloves. The equipment is evidently intended for a long journey, probably on horseback.

[1] The similarity to the costume of the ancient Assyrian priests is arresting. A splendid series of pictures of shamans' costumes will be found in Holmberg, *Finno-Ugrian and Siberian Mythology* (Boston, Mass., 1927).

THE ARTIFICIAL REGULATION OF ECSTASY 59

Among the shamans of the Altai Tatars, the mantic accessories almost amount to a scenario.

Certain external conditions are helpful and even necessary to the seer. The first requisite is solitude and quiet, for purposes of concentration. A large proportion of seers have been drawn from the shepherd class all over Europe and Asia. But the solitude may be artificially produced, e.g. by closing the eyes, or covering the head. The silence of those around is a great help to the seer.

The chief feature which distinguishes European manticism from that of Asia and Polynesia is the absence of early record in Europe of drum, dance, and dramatic representation. European mantic poetry is generally accompanied only by the human voice. Othin, the *thulr*, the mantic god, has no musical instrument; he never dances. So also the Irish *filid*, and the Welsh mantic poets.[1] Musical instruments and dance are similarly lacking from Sanskrit manticism. We have seen that the intellectual preoccupations and speculations of the Sanskrit seers bear a striking resemblance to those of the seers of ancient Thrace and Gaul. Can we trace in these features elements in the channel of mantic thought from East to West across Southern Eurasia?

In Northern Asia and in Polynesia, in contrast to Europe, drum, dance and drama are among the most prominent and general accompaniments of modern man-

[1] Traces of music are not wholly lacking in Celtic mantic tradition. We may refer to the story of the musical branch which Cormac MacAirt acquired in Tír Tairngaire (Stokes, *Irische Texte*, III, pp. 183 ff.), and to the 'birds of Rhiannon' referred to in medieval Welsh literature, notably the *Mabinogi of Branwen*, and the *Triads* (*Myvyrian Archaeology*, p. 899, no. 29); cf. further *The Book of Taliesin*, XLVIII, l. 31 (ed. Skene, *Four Ancient Books of Wales*).

ticism, and it is largely the prominence of these features which has led many scholars to overlook the intellectual side of the seers' activities. Clearly Polynesian and Asiatic manticism have flowed in kindred channels, which for many hundreds of years have been alien to those of European thought; but they have not always been wholly alien. The *nekuia* in the *Odyssey*—the account of Odysseus's journey to the land of the dead to consult the seer Teiresias—as well as the stories of Persephone and of Alcestis, bear a strange resemblance to the journeys of the Tatar shaman, the Dyak seeress, the Polynesian divine heroes, the Japanese gods, and the Assyrian goddess Ishtar, to the Underworld to seek the souls of the dead. The theme, as we shall see, is as ancient as Assyrian poetry, probably as old as Sumerian; and it is still popular. At the same time, it is important to note that while the modern shamanism of Northern and Central Asia gives such paramount importance to drum and dance, the traditional oral narrative poetry of the Yenisei Tatars which deals extensively with spiritual matters is wholly ignorant of both.[1]

Perhaps the aspect of manticism for which evidence fails us most signally is in regard to the mental processes by which the seer passes into his ecstasy, through it, and out of it, and how far dissociation takes place. We have seen that in the best recorded displays of even the most backward peoples the seer during ecstasy is able to compose extempore and recite an elaborate poetical composition. And it is important to emphasise the seer's

[1] I have discussed this subject more fully in a paper on 'Shamanism among the Tatars of Central Asia' in the *Journal of the Royal Anthropological Institute*, vol. LXVI (1936); see pp. 110 f.

THE ARTIFICIAL REGULATION OF ECSTASY

perfect mastery and control, not only of his artistic material, but also of his own movements (see above). He knows exactly how far to go in his spiritual journey, when to stop, and how to prepare himself and his audiences for the return to the material world. This in itself suggests that the seer's mental condition is healthy and 'safe'.

How far the seer produces poetry when at the height of his ecstasy is one of the questions which we should most wish to see answered. The evidence is insufficient at present to be conclusive. But so far as this evidence goes, it suggests that when the ecstasy is at its height, the poetry ceases.[1] In Uganda, when the royal mediums practise a form of trance which appears to be unregulated, and when total dissociation appears to take place, no poetry is spoken. Yet other poets in the same area, bearing the external signs of professional dissociation, compose and recite extempore poetry.[2] It would seem that poetry, that is, eloquence and music combined, is the language of prayer and spell, and of all communication between

---

[1] I am aware that many statements could be cited to the contrary. Thus Kagwa tells us (*The Customs of the Baganda*, p. 115) that Mukasa's *mandwa* 'recited' a 'chant' during 'her prophecy'; but, in quoting her cry, he gives only a single line, after which he tells us drums were beaten and 'after quiet had been restored she would begin her prophecy'. Her words are not given. Castagné tells us (*op. cit.* p. 94) that the *bakshas* of the Kazak-Kirghiz recited an invocation to the spirits during the 'phase décisive de surexcitation extrême', but he is summarising a work by Levanevski, and the evidence on this point is not clear. The Vedda shaman, as reported by the Seligmans, *The Veddas*, pp. 218 ff., appears to have gone into ecstasy after the chanting, not during it, in every instance. On the other hand instances in which the chant precedes the ecstasy are too numerous to require citation here; but see Kagwa, *op. cit.* p. 127. See also p. 29 above.

[2] See Grant, *op. cit.* p. 183.

THE MANTIC TECHNIQUE

human beings and spirits. At the moment when the divine spirit enters the seer in response to his summons, when this spirit actually 'possesses' the seer, he ceases, in his own opinion and that of his auditors, to speak from his own intellect, or by his own art, and speaks as another. In Uganda this is certainly so. In Polynesia it is so. And it would seem to be so among the Turkish peoples. Once more we may ask, Is this the birth of drama? Is this why ecstasy and inspiration are so constantly associated with contact between the seer and the dead? Is this why the birth of drama is so constantly associated with the tombs of the dead?

Generally speaking it will, I think, be found that the extent to which the seer becomes withdrawn into a condition of dissociation or trance is in inverse proportion to the amount of regulation which controls his ecstatic periods. Among the Tatars ecstasy appears to have become largely an official procedure; among the Tungus to some extent a matter of technique. When the Altai shaman performs his elaborately extemporised dramatic journey to Heaven at the annual tribal sacrifice, his faculties must be alert, his self-control and self-direction complete. But we must beware against facile generalisation in this matter. The Tatars tell us that though all their shamans can mount into the air, only the greatest shamans can reach as high as to the sixteenth Heaven. Does this mean that only a few of their great contemplatives have sufficient power of concentration to divest themselves completely of all consciousness of their material surroundings? This must be particularly difficult to do when conducting a great tribal sacrifice; yet there is probably no occasion when, in native opinion, immediate

Plate 1. Buryat Shaman (*front view*)

THE ARTIFICIAL REGULATION OF ECSTASY

contact between man and the highest god is so necessary. We cannot doubt that complete dissociation takes place upon occasion, even among these highly developed people. It has already been mentioned that even the *knout* of the Cossack has failed to arouse a Tatar shaman from his ecstasy, while it is said that the Koryak sometimes beat their shaman severely during ecstasy in order 'to test the sincerity of his professions and the genuineness of his revelations'.[1] There is perhaps no aspect of shamanism for which we await with so much eager expectation the conclusions of the psychologists who alone are competent to interpret the evidence on this matter.

It is commonly insisted on by experts that the shaman recites in a condition of dissociation more or less complete what he has previously soaked in during daily life. The mind, moving on traditional lines, reproduces unconsciously what it has previously assimilated. There seems to be little doubt that this is partially the case, at least in certain instances. But where and when, one wonders, could the Tatar shaman have acquired the knowledge and the art revealed in his extempore songs, or practised to such perfection the dance and the ventriloquial displays which he performs in his ecstasy?[2] The literary and ethnographical evidence suggests rather that they are the result of extreme concentration at the time of performance. The stimulants have put him into a condition of mental exaltation, so that he is at concert pitch, in a

[1] Kennan, *op. cit.* p. 209.
[2] Radlov, *Aus Sibirien*, vol. II, p. 57. For a fuller discussion of this question in relation to the shaman's performance I may perhaps refer to my paper on 'Shamanism among the Tatars of Central Asia', *Journal of the Royal Anthropological Institute*, vol. LXVI (1936), p. 101.

more elevated frame of mind than his fellows. That is to say, he sheds their immediate preoccupations. As a result his imagination is released in the world of speculation. The period of quiet preparation has been utilised by the mind to think away the immediate and the material as much as to reinstate itself in another environment. This process of thinking away, shedding the consciousness of environment, is incomplete where dissociation is incomplete. But the material world has been removed to the outer verge of consciousness. The focus is on spiritual things.

There has been a tendency among European writers[1] to regard the transport of mantic persons as due to pathological causes—as a symptom of hysteria or some other nervous disease; or at best as a safety-valve for those afflicted with epilepsy or the like. Yet the widespread nature of the phenomenon over the greater part of the world, its ancient history, its association with many great names, and the respect in which the seer is held in the communities who know him intimately should, I think, give us reason to doubt the soundness of these explanations, and it is interesting to note that among recent writers Shirokogoroff especially emphasises the fact that the shaman must be an essentially healthy person.[2] Among foreign scholars there is a growing tendency to stress the intellectual and the artistic achievements of the seer. A more extensive knowledge among ethnologists of the languages of the primitive and backward peoples among whom manticism is still a living institu-

1 E.g. Czaplicka, *Aboriginal Siberia, passim.*
2 'It is necessary to note that the shaman must be a healthy person.... The shaman can not let himself fall into a nervous fit': *loc. cit.*

Plate 2. Buryat Shaman in ecstasy, and wearing bird costume

tion, and some more records of the actual words spoken by seers during ecstasy, would doubtless greatly strengthen this view. It is much to be hoped that no effort will be spared to collect such records before it is too late.

In every country where heroic or commercial conditions prevail there must exist, alongside these elements, a contemplative element. The contemplative elements, finding conditions against them in active life, develop for themselves, with the help of traditional technique, a way of life which permits the normal and healthy use of the contemplative faculty. Heroic and contemplative alike tend to develop on pathological lines in adverse social conditions. As instances of the former we may point to the *berserkir* of early Norse literature, or to those who run amuck among the Malay and other eastern peoples. As regards the pathological development of contemplative subjects, there is, of course, no doubt whatever that nervous diseases are especially prevalent in Northern Siberia; and it will be readily conceded that nervous and highly strung people make likely subjects for ecstasy and other forms of manticism. That people who, according to Siberian standards, are actually mentally abnormal or diseased, make good shamans has yet to be shown.[1] Nor have I found satisfactory evidence elsewhere that people who are obviously mentally diseased are held in high esteem for mantic gifts in their own community.

In the meantime much light could undoubtedly be

---

[1] Shirokogoroff holds the view—the result of a wide knowledge and experience of Tungus and other eastern Asiatic forms of shamanism—that good health and great strength are the first requisite of a shaman: *loc. cit.*

thrown on our subject by a consideration of inspiration in our own area, where conditions of life are familiar to us, where the 'inspired' are drawn from among ourselves, and where the literary records are exceptionally full and valuable. I am referring to the Monastic Orders. It may be said that the results of Greek culture gradually dispelled contemplation as a profession from Southern Europe. But the religious orders of the Middle Ages represent a reaction and a return. In particular, the technique by which the contemplative life is followed by the Carmelite nuns of our own day, who are perhaps the most contemplative of all religious orders in Europe, is interesting and important. Here the process of stripping away all that would distract from prayer is achieved by the enclosure wall and a bare cell, and by absolute silence. By this means the mental disturbances, the accidental word or event, so disintegrating to constructive thought, are reduced to a minimum. The immediate and the material are gradually shifted to the outer verge of consciousness. The mind gradually trains itself by a definite technique, taught and acquired by recognised processes, to a loving attention upon God. Gradually the human spirit learns to live in our material world only painfully and temporarily, sojourning mainly in the world of spirit. In some of the more accomplished or spiritually minded, consciousness of the material world becomes secondary, and at times appears to be lost altogether. These people are not usually called upon to reveal their experiences in literary form. Instances of such literary composition are, however, not rare, as the works of the medieval mystics show. And the writings of St Teresa in particular show us how effectively this can be done. *The Interior Castle*—a great romance of the soul—shows once more the close connection between inspiration and literary beauty.

It seems to me that the Carmelite evidence is of special value in regard to the questions (1) how far the 'call' of the seer and his tendency to ecstasy are to be regarded as pathological, and (2) how far total dissociation takes place. In regard to the first question there can, I think, be little doubt that a nervous and highly strung, sensitive temperament is a natural foundation for a contemplative postulant.[1] But it may safely be said that an abnormal or unhealthy-minded postulant would not be accepted, and any symptom of hysteria or unhealthy mental condition among members of the Order is treated with sound common sense. That is to say, the patient is put under the care of a doctor and a nurse. A quick and ever-present sense of humour is one of the most noticeable features of the members of this Order. It is enjoined on the novices by the senior members of the Order that a nun who makes the sisters laugh during the hour of recreation is the one who confers the greatest benefit on the little community.

In regard to our second question, the testimony of St Teresa's writings leaves little room to doubt that Trance, or total dissociation, takes place. Ecstasy may be, and doubtless is, rare, even here; and how common, and with what degree of completeness dissociation is practised is known fully only to members of the Order. But we know that what we may vulgarly call ecstasy or

[1] Not infrequently people enter this Order after a nervous breakdown. This does not mean that the nervous system is disordered at the time of entry. It is natural that people who have the gift of living a life of silent contemplation will break down in the disintegrating rush of modern active life, especially town life.

trance is the consummation of which *The Way of Perfection*, *The Interior Castle*, and even the *Life of St Teresa*, form the graded record of personal preparation and experience, and afford the technique and mental discipline for her followers. From these it appears that the question of dissociation is one of degree. The youngest novice who practises the daily discipline of silent contemplation is using the first means towards dissociation.[1] But it is the normal exercise of a healthy faculty, resulting in a poised and balanced outlook, and a ready laugh. And this is natural. For the faculties, elsewhere heavily embroiled in the struggle for existence, have been on holiday, the soul has been freed for a spell from the insistence of the present, and has returned refreshed and rested, and correspondingly clear-sighted.

Actually the healthy mental condition of the enclosed, silent, contemplative Carmelites cannot be doubted by anyone who has read the works of St Teresa, or had any experience of the Order. Her own critical faculty and balanced judgment, and especially her common sense, are acknowledged by everyone competent to judge, and she herself distinguishes so sharply between hysteria and genuine mental contemplation and ecstasy that we—at least such of us as have only an outside knowledge of these matters—must accept her judgment. She had abundant experience of observing both the unhealthy and the healthy mental life, and on this matter she knew better than we can do. However expert psychologists explain

[1] It is now generally held, I believe, by Carmelite nuns that ecstasy and trance are closely bound up with nationality, and are by no means either universal or evenly distributed throughout the Order, nor are they believed to be wholly dependent on temperament, training, or discipline.

the phenomena, we must accept the facts as she gives them. To do otherwise would be, it seems to me, an impertinence. It would be to accord to a literary genius who offers us the results of a lifetime's experience less respect than we accord to the most indifferent practical ethnologist.

It may seem that all this is a long way from poetic inspiration and the trance of seer or medium. Yet the study of the most contemplative of our orders is relevant, and has much to teach us about the side of manticism which is perhaps the most difficult of all to acquire information about—the education, discipline, and preparation of the seer for his mantic inspiration. In the first place, it is a striking testimony to the absence of any connection between race on the one hand and heredity and the tendency to manticism on the other; and also to the predominant part played by economic conditions in the production of seers.—Before 1914 there were at most three reformed Carmelite convents in this country. Shortly after the war there were about thirty-seven. It teaches us the kind of person attracted by the contemplative life. It assures us of their sound mental and nervous condition, while—I think—emphasising their tendency to 'nerviness' in uncongenial, i.e. in active life. It teaches us something of the leaders of this class of thought. And here it is interesting to note the chief characteristics attributed to St Teresa by those whose attitude was alien from our own, her biographers themselves men in religious orders. Chief among these are her extreme power of concentration,[1] her great intellectual

1 *The Interior Castle* (English translation by the Benedictines of Stanbrook, 3rd ed., London, 1921), p. 10.

power,[1] her fine literary style,[2] her strong common sense.[3] We may also add her sense of humour.[4] Not the least interesting aspects of her visionary works from our point of view are the traditional character of their mould, the affinities of her literary forms and formulae[5] with those of other great writers, such as St Thomas Aquinas on the one hand, and with Dante on the other.

One of the greatest difficulties which one has to try to overcome in reading the writings of St Teresa and of the other medieval mystics is that of really understanding what she is talking about. The vocabulary is our own, the diction is familiar, but the mould, the literary formulae, are alien to the traditional mould in which modern secular thought is cast. The familiar words and formulae are symbols for unfamiliar ideas. How much more must this be so when we seek to interpret the utterances of a Chuckchee shaman! How little qualified are we to know the traditional, as distinct from the lexicographical value of word and phrase, to interpret the traditional figurative diction—to know when a shaman does not intend us to place a literal interpretation on his words! The paucity of our information on mantic matters is constantly brought home to us. But this is only half the story, and the wide margin of error in the interpretation of such material as we possess is less generally realised. For instances we may turn to certain books of incantation current among the Mussulman *bakshas* which make mention of Turkish saints who mount on lions, dragons, etc., while similar feats are attributed to many notable characters of the ancient Mussulman

1 *The Interior Castle*, p. 29. 2 *Ib.* p. 33; 3 *Ib.* p. 27.
4 See e.g. *The Way of Perfection*, English translation by the Benedictines of Stanbrook (London, 1911), pp 14, 146. 5 *Ib.* p. 30.

THE ARTIFICIAL REGULATION OF ECSTASY

world. But it is clear from the oral literature current among the Tatars of Central Asia to-day that identical feats are there attributed to the heroes and heroines in a manner which shows that they are to be understood as among, not the actual, but the spiritual experiences of these people. As a typical instance of the literal interpretation of ritual symbolism by those ignorant of its true significance we may refer to the statement made of a great Mongol shaman of the time of Jenghiz Khan who is said to have counted among his other 'prodigies' (*prodigues*) that of having ascended to Heaven on his horse—clearly a typical piece of shamanist ritual,[1] such as that performed symbolically by the Buryat shaman on his *ongon*, or 'hobby-horse'. Stadling tells us[2] that in the oral literature of the Yakut a special diction is used consisting of three times as many words as those in current daily use, and that figurative imagery is largely employed, making such literary diction 'practically untranslatable'.

There can be no doubt that a study of medieval mysticism, with its stress on ecstasy, would be a most valuable corrective to many misconceptions which are inevitable while our studies are limited to inspiration among peoples of alien language, alien traditions, and alien race. Such a study would, I think, go far to prove that contemplation, culminating in ecstasy, is not a pathological condition,[3] but a normal development of

---
[1] See Köprülüzade Mehmed Fuad, 'Influence du Chamanisme Turco-Mongol sur les Ordres Mystiques Musulmans', *Mémoires de l'Institut de Turcologie de l'Université de Stamboul* (New Series), vol. 1 (Istanboul, 1929).
[2] *Loc. cit.*
[3] Nervous diseases are very prevalent in eastern Siberia. The Tungus are especially susceptible to epilepsy. It is natural, therefore, that the Tungus shamans should be affected to some extent. But in general the shamans are said to be healthy people, and mentally superior to their neighbours. See K. Donner, *Sibirien*, p. 230; cf. Shirokogoroff, *loc. cit.*

certain healthy faculties, which are scarcely able to function in modern civilised communities, where the emphasis is on practical activity, and where the population tends to be congested. The study of religious trance would certainly disprove the theory that vacuity has any part in the mind of shaman or of seer. At the same time it would help us to understand the necessity for periods of silence felt by all mantic persons.—That during this silence they are not only occupied in thinking away their material surroundings, but also in focusing on spiritual and intellectual matters. It would teach us something of the graded stages, technically scheduled, by which the shaman or the seer educates himself for his trance.

The ultimate pronouncement on the condition of the mind of the seer during ecstasy must, of course, lie with the psychologists. But empirically the seer is known by his works; and a comparison of a number of the best specimens in backward communities such as Northern and Central Asia and Polynesia, where ecstasy is highly esteemed and cultivated, leaves little room to doubt that seers are generally the best intellects of their own *milieus*. The chief criterion is the oral literary works which they have themselves composed, and which they have inspired, either directly, or as originators of the literary tradition. A study of the oral literature of those portions of the Old World where writing was unknown until our own day leaves little room to doubt that the poetry of the seer has been the most important factor in the history of human thought.

CHAPTER V

RITUAL AND MAGIC, AND THEIR RELATIONSHIP TO THE MANTIC TRADITION

THE evidence afforded by the comparative study of the oral literature of peoples on the periphery of the civilised world, like the Tatars and the Polynesians, suggests that the attitude of their priests and seers towards ritual does not differ greatly from our own. The emphasis in spiritual matters is placed on the rite, rather than on the ritual; on close relations between the shaman or tohunga and the supernatural power with whom he humbly seeks contact, rather than on the procedure and observances by means of which this contact is obtained. As a famous Yakut shaman once told Sieroszewski, the outward signs of his communion with spirits, the dance and drum, and ventriloquial performance, are not regarded very seriously, even by the audience. 'A true shaman is recognised by his spiritual gifts.'[1] The ritual would seem to be largely a means of attuning the mind for the performance of the rite, whether by suggestion or instruction. These spiritual leaders do not arrogate to themselves the power of the gods by their ritual performances. This is often done by their ignorant successors, who follow their formulae without understanding their purpose. Even in our oral 'texts' the distinction between religion and magic is often obscured. It is not always

[1] Sieroszewski, *Revue de l'Histoire des Religions*, vol. XVI (1902), pp. 318 f.

easy to distinguish hymns and prayers from spells, blessings and curses from charms, or to know when a ritual is intended and believed to be *immediately* efficacious. But in general a comparative study of these oral 'texts' suggests that magic plays a relatively unimportant part among the native learned classes, and that it has a greater hold on the lower than on the higher classes of religious thinkers, though it may be cultivated by the latter in sanctuaries for the sake of popular appeal.

Wherever we have oral texts relating to native learning, the connection between ritual and learning is found to be very close. And wherever ritual is performed by specialists, such as priests or seers, the native learning is in the hands of the same class, and associated with the great sanctuaries, which among unlettered peoples seem usually to be the chief centres of learning. It is usual to find that this native learned class utilises great religious festivals as an opportunity for giving instruction and education, not only in religious matters, but in secular matters also. Indeed we have seen that in general among unlettered peoples no distinction is made between religious and secular learning. Among the Polynesians all knowledge is *tapu*. The great sanctuary of Raiatea in the Central Pacific was the chief repository of the native oral records relating to scientific discoveries, and to historical, especially genealogical learning. Even among the Galla of East Africa, at the great annual feast of Atete, the priest drills the people in what we may call elementary nature study as a part of the ritual:

Priest: 'O Wonder. O Wonder.'
People: 'What are the wonders?'
Priest: 'The water runs without being urged; the earth

THEIR RELATIONSHIP TO MANTIC TRADITION

is fixed without pegs; the Heavens hold themselves up without supports; in the firmament God has sown the stars. These things fill me with wonder. Let us all pray to God,'[1] etc.

Galla ritual practice evidently requires that the attention of the people shall be called to the wonders of Creation before they are asked to praise the Creator.

Owing to the absence of ancient sanctuaries, with their vested interests in traditional learning, colonial countries like Iceland in the Viking Age and Maori New Zealand are comparatively poor in the more elaborate forms of ritual. But magic flourished in both. Anyone who would attempt to write an account of Icelandic ritual from the evidence of the sagas would have a barren row to hoe; but the sagas abound in spicy passages of witchcraft and magic. The poverty of ritual cannot be attributed to lack of religious fervour in either country. New Zealand had an extensive pantheon of popular gods, and there were plenty of *tohungas*, or priestly seers. In Iceland nearly every chief of consequence was also a *gothi*, or priest, and had a temple of his own. And both countries developed a phenomenal wealth of historical traditions. The poverty of ritual seems to be attributable in both cases to the weakening of the ancient sanctuary traditions, some of which the learned Icelander Snorri sought to recapture later, during the thirteenth century.

It is precisely these oral traditions, preserved largely in the sanctuaries, which alone make ritual intelligible; and with the loss of tradition ritual must inevitably deteriorate into magic, and ultimately into a meaningless

[1] Cerulli, 'The Folk Literature of the Galla of Southern Abyssinia', *Harvard African Studies*, III (Cambridge, Mass. 1922), p. 137.

set of actions or a game.[1] It is quite in accordance with the religious beliefs of the Mongol Buryat that their shamans during their religious ceremonies mount up to Heaven symbolically on a hobby-horse; and at the annual tribal sacrifice the skin and head of a horse are symbolically raised up towards Heaven on a pole. The symbolism is a logical outcome of Buryat religious traditions, and is probably ultimately connected in some remote way with the great sacrifice of the horse of which we hear in the ancient Indian epic the *Mahabharata*. But in Norway in the Viking Age we read of Egill Skallagrímsson raising a horse's head on a pole and turning it to all four corners of the Heavens in order to lay a curse on his enemy by frightening the spirits of the land.[2] It is obvious that the rite must originally have been derived from the east, for it is unlikely that ancient rites connected with the horse could originate in a country like Norway. Most likely they have passed through Sweden, which in ancient times specialised in horse-breeding, and which at all times carried on a lively trade across the Baltic and down the Volga. It is clear, however, that whatever its origin the rite had become a purely magical one in Norway. All trace of its original function as a means of transport for the shaman has been lost. It is interesting to note that the Mongols also have a habit of raising horses' heads and skins on poles as a part of their ritual, while Kennan also notes a custom among the Yurak of erecting dogs' heads and skins on poles for magical purposes.[3]

[1] For a view different from the one which I have expressed the reader may refer to Lord Raglan, *Jocasta's Crime* (London, 1933), p. 88 ff.
[2] *Egils Saga Skallagrímssonar*, ch. 57.   [3] *Tent Life in Siberia*, p. 209.

Plate 3. Oirot Horse Sacrifice

The special function of the seer as a repository of ancient traditions has an important bearing on the part played by ritual; for ritual, it seems, cannot flourish divorced from tradition. Yet it does not develop out of tradition. The native oral historical traditions of Uganda owe their preservation largely to the peculiar form of ritual associated with the dead kings of the country, which provided for every king after death a medium, a temple, and a court maintained nominally in perpetuity; a kind of permanent drama, and surely a very remarkable type of public record office. In the neighbouring country of Ankole, where no such ritual prevailed, there are practically no historical traditions. In Polynesia the ritual dramas have been of the utmost importance as a means of preserving the traditions of the past. This is very far from suggesting that these traditions, and more especially the historical traditions, necessarily owe their origin to the ritual. Both the traditions and the ritual have their origin in some common source. How do they arise? What is their purpose?

On the whole the evidence of oral literature seems to suggest that the elaboration of ritual, as distinct from a simple rite, is primarily an attempt to stimulate the imagination. Elaborate ritual is generally performed by a specialist, such as a priest or a seer. The means by which he stimulates the imagination of the assembly most effectively is that of increasing their knowledge, so as to enable them to apprehend more fully some truth of which he believes himself to be in possession. He may demonstrate by mimesis, or teach orally. We have seen that the Baganda mediums of the animal gods make their appeal through the eye, by assuming the rôle of the animal in question, roaring like a lion; turning the head and snapping like a crocodile; growling like a leopard; crawling and wriggling like a python. In Polynesia, as we shall see, ritual drama keeps the people well informed of the stories of the gods and of the flight of divine heroes to Heaven. The ritual flight of the soul to Heaven is sometimes reduced to a symbol, as, for example, in certain temple ceremonies on the Island of Bali,[1] where it is represented by a gigantic kite. But in many cases little or no appeal is made to the eye in ritual, and then we are soon over the border line into tradition. A type of recital which illustrates very clearly the border line between ritual and tradition is *The Song of the Dyak Head Feast* among the Sea Dyaks of North Borneo, which I shall refer to again later.

The actual knowledge by which the performer of a ritual seeks to stimulate the imagination of the assembly may be either subjective, that is to say, esoteric or religious; or it may be objective, whether scientific or historical. If it is subjective or religious, we call its verbal transmission a myth.[2] If it is objective, that is, scientific or historical, we say it is handed on by tradition.

The relationship of ritual to science and history, and the process by which it deteriorates into magic when divorced from its accompanying tradition, is easily traceable in Polynesia, where our oral records are exceptionally full and well preserved. The *karakias* or chants,

---

[1] A picture of one of these ceremonies and the giant kite is given in my paper on 'The Kite. A Study in Polynesian Tradition' in *Journal of the Royal Anthropological Institute*, vol. LXI (1931), Plate LVI.

[2] For a useful collection of definitions of the word 'myth' by various scholars, see Lord Raglan, *The Hero* (London, 1936), pp. 128 ff.

which are regarded by the ignorant among the natives themselves as controlling the weather, are often merely the memoranda of the more intelligent *tohungas*, and enumerate the winds which blow on a certain coast, or the various types of waves which must be encountered on a certain voyage. The so-called magic calabash of the winds, which finds constant mention in the oral traditions, is simply a practical working instrument of combined sextant and compass. Genealogies sung by mothers as charms to their babies owe their origin to the elaborate ritual with which genealogies are chanted at great festivals held specially for the purpose, such as we find in the Marquesas. But this ritual in its turn owes its origin to the need of a great seafaring people who have no written charters or wills to preserve a sound oral record of their claims and their rights to succession. Their long absences from home, and the chances of death abroad, developed genealogical lore into a science, just as in Iceland in the Viking Age, and with precisely similar results.

The relationship of ritual to historical tradition, as distinct from such scientific knowledge, and its deterioration into a magical charm, are seen very clearly in the texts of certain wind charms of the Moriori of the Chatham Islands. These charms are known as Tawhakis,[1] and their connection with the hero Tawhaki, who figures prominently in the greatest Cycle of Polynesian tradition,[2] is preserved both in their name, and in the

---

[1] See the collection by Shand, *Journal of the Polynesian Society*, vol. VII, pp. 75 ff.
[2] I have given a summary of the traditions relating to Tawhaki in *The Growth of Literature*, vol. III, pp. 272 f.

character of their contents. Polynesian genealogies place Tawhaki, the most illustrious *ariki* ancestor of Polynesia, about A.D. 700. His fame rests largely on his ascent to the highest Heaven through some sixteen superimposed Heavens, where he becomes immortal. In order to perform this feat successfully he has first to visit his grandmother in the bowels of the earth.

Another great Polynesian hero is Maui,[1] who also seeks to win immortality by creeping through his mother, hoping to emerge reborn. But Maui failed to emerge and died, though a tradition from Rarotonga tells us that the feat was successfully performed by an *ariki*.

These two great Cycles of tradition must surely contain reminiscences of Hindu funeral practices, as we see them in Bali to-day. Indeed it is possible that the stories originated in such a ritual. In Bali a *kshatriya*, or man of princely caste, is carried to the summit of a many-storied tower for cremation (sometimes eleven stories),[2] while a man of non-*kshatriya* caste is cremated in the interior of a wooden bull, or more rarely some other animal. It may be said that, like Maui, they enter never to emerge. Again we read of the heir to the throne of Trevandrum, the capital of Travancore in South-West India, entering a golden cow in the temple as a part of the coronation ceremony, after which he was blessed by the Brahmins.[3]

It would seem probable that the Hindu temple ceremony, which has survived as an important piece of national ritual in the conservative region of South-West

[1] See *Growth*, loc. cit.
[2] Friedrich, *Journal of the Asiatic Society*, vol. IX (New Series, 1877), p. 93.
[3] See S. Mateer, *The Land of Charity* (London, 1871), pp. 169 ff.

THEIR RELATIONSHIP TO MANTIC TRADITION

India, was carried to Bali and, of course, elsewhere during the period of the great Hindu empire of Java about the eighth century, and has survived in the form of legends attached to the early heroes Maui and Tawhaki. I do not mean by this suggestion to lend support to the general view that Maui or Tawhaki were historical persons. The value of Tawhaki's date, which is fairly well established on the Polynesian pedigrees, is that it suggests that this circle of ideas radiated over the Pacific from Southern Asia, at the time when the great Hindu empire in Indonesia was at its height, and certainly before the Mohammedan conquest early in the fifteenth century. The Hindu ritual of India, which spread in early times to Bali, has radiated out as heroic tradition to heathen Polynesia. The last faint ripple is preserved as a magical formula in the lonely Chatham Islands.[1]

It is, of course, not difficult in any case to trace the origin of a ritual which manifestly arises from scientific knowledge or a historical fact, or, as a secondary development, from an antiquarian speculation, and to watch its deterioration, with the loss of tradition, into a magical formula.[2] But are we justified in supposing other forms of religious ritual with their accompanying tradition to be of similar origin? Let us turn to the ritual of the Tatar shaman. This will be found to be in close relationship with a vast body of Tatar mythological tradition which has found expression in the narrative poetry of the

[1] I have treated this subject somewhat more fully in *The Growth of Literature*, vol. III, pp. 302 ff.
[2] The close association of magic with science is admitted by Professor Rose who, postulating a savage working magic to make the rain fall, says: 'This, being in intention practical, is a sort of bastard sister of applied science': *Handbook of Greek Mythology* (London, 1928), p. 11.

Kirghiz and the Yenisei Tatars. Here we find supernatural journeys to the Heavens and the Underworld which are portrayed with the same concrete detail and paraphernalia as in the well-known ritual sacrifice of the Altai shaman, and the journey of the Yakut shaman to conduct the dead to the Underworld. The journeys to the Heavens are, in their details and *mise-en-scène*, strikingly like those of Tawhaki and other Polynesian heroes, and similar ones are to be found in the Japanese chronicles written in the eighth century—another peripheral country. Are these similarities accidental? Can they possibly have arisen as an invention, a piece of religious ritual created in Siberia from the shaman's imagination, an idle tale in the Pacific to amuse the islanders? I do not think so. The journeys to the Underworld, both in Asia and in the Pacific, may well be a remote reflection of the great Indian cave temples of Ajanta and the days of King Aṣoka; but they have made many halts on their march northwards—in Gandhara on the Indus in the days of King Kanishka; and in the middle distance there are the great cave temples of the Uigurs of Turkestan, again at their height in the seventh century. The link with Japan is suggested by the great Korean cave temples of the same phase. Similar caves, with elaborate concrete furniture of the spirit world, are still used in Tibet by the living in a way which invites comparison with the ritual of the Tatar shaman, and the mythological traditions of Tatar narrative poetry.

It has been claimed that the Babylonian Epic of Creation, which was recited as a part of the New Year Ritual, was originally composed to have a magical virtue, that all Babylonian mythology is magical in purpose, and

Plate 4. Temple Buildings, Kyzyl, Chinese Turkestan

that this claim is even relevant to the question of the origin of *Gilgamesh*.[1] These are questions which I must leave to specialists; but it is fair to say that while it is very usual elsewhere to find both narrative poetry and prose recited during great religious festivals, they are not necessarily to be considered as forming any part of the religious ceremony proper. Thus we learn from the Icelandic saga of Harold Hardrada that when the king was keeping the Christmas festival at Trondhjem, he engaged an Icelander with a good reputation as a saga teller to entertain the court every night with a saga which related the king's exploits. This was, of course, after the church services. It is interesting to note that the king tells the Icelander at the outset that he must make his story-telling last over the twelve days of Yule; and each day the king stops him after a certain time, so as to make the story last out. At great religious feasts dignified and relevant entertainment out of hours must always have formed an important element in the programme, and been a great stimulus to artistic production. Very possibly it may account for the growth of epic length, and it certainly accounts for the political or religious bias of many epic poems. Their value for religious instruction and propaganda must have been very generally recognised; but I know of nothing in the literature of ancient Europe or modern Asia or Polynesia to suggest that they have any connection with magic.

Our great difficulty is to distinguish the purpose for which a certain type of poem originated from the secondary purpose to which it may be put. It is often

[1] See the chapter by C. J. Gadd on 'Babylonian Myth and Ritual' in *Myth and Ritual*, ed. by Prof. S. H. Hooke (Oxford, 1933), p. 62.

even more difficult to distinguish the introduction into a poem of what has aptly been called a minor myth from the utilisation of the traditional poetic diction associated with such a myth in a totally different setting. The opening of a certain Anglo-Saxon charm against a sudden pain[1] consists of some narrative lines relating to the ride of valkyries through the air, and passes immediately to an invocation to a spear to leave the wound. But the charm is not a charm against a spear wound, but against a sudden pain or stitch. I believe that the sharp stab of the stitch suggested comparison with a spear wound; and that the introduction of the valkyries is probably merely a piece of figurative poetic diction due to the association of ideas in the mind of a polished poet versed in the mythological conceptions and allusions of his day, as our own poets refer to Shakespeare and the Muses. It would be a mistake to invert the history of the form and suppose that the myth of the valkyries, or the convention of celbrating them in poetical form, arose as a magical formula or had a magical origin. The many prose and poetical passages in early Norse literature in which they occur prove that the case is quite the contrary.

The Song of the Dyak Head Feast chanted by the Sea Dyaks of North Borneo[2] is a more difficult question, for while the ritual itself is directed to invite the great war god, Singalang Burong, to be present at their feast, to

[1] A critical text is published by Wülcker, *Bibliothek der Angelsächsischen Poesie* (Kassel, 1883), vol. I, p. 317. The text is also published by Sedgefield, *An Anglo-Saxon Book of Verse and Prose* (Manchester, 1928), p. 357.
[2] See Perham's papers in the *Journal of the Straits Branch of the Royal Asiatic Society*, vol. II (1878), pp. 123 ff. See also Ling Roth, *The Natives of Sarawak and British North Borneo*, vol. II, pp. 174 ff.

celebrate the taking of a human head, the form which the ritual takes is that of the recital of a head feast of the past given by the great Dyak mythical hero Klieng to which Singalang Burong was invited. As the Dyaks sing of Klieng's feast—and many of those present take part in the chanting—they perform the corresponding ceremonial, and offer their own homage to Singalang Burong in accordance with it. The recital is calculated to ensure the handing on to all present of the ancient story of Klieng's relations with the god, and to attune rightly the minds of those present by the recital of relevant matter in archaic exalted diction. Nothing in the text of this particular recital suggests that the words have a compelling force.

But the educational value and function of ritual, whether by demonstration or by recital, is perhaps best illustrated from the ritual performances of the *arioi* of Tahiti and kindred societies elsewhere in the Pacific, such as the *hoki* of the Marquesas. Here we have great seasonal festivals, accompanied by public demonstrations. These demonstrations, as given by the *arioi*, have been interpreted as fertility rites; for a part of the performances consisted of a demonstration of the union of the god Tangaroa with matter, and the creation of man, consequent upon this union. But this was only one item in their programme, and there can be no doubt that it has come to take a disproportionate place in our estimate of the *arioi*, owing to the dismay with which such practices were viewed by early European observers.[1] It is im-

[1] Even in our own day Sir J. G. Frazer calls them 'a licentious fraternity of strolling players and mountebanks': *The Belief in Immortality and the Worship of the Dead*, vol. II (London, 1913), p. 259.

portant for us to bear in mind that the *arioi* were held in the highest esteem by the better informed of the Polynesians themselves, and numbered in their ranks some of the highest chiefs and priests. The fact that all *arioi* women except those of the highest rank were compelled to destroy their offspring hardly suggests a fertility rite.

Now if we examine the *arioi* programme, and compare it with the repertoires of analogous societies from various groups in the Pacific, it becomes clear, I think, that these performances constitute an elaborate historical pageant. The repertoire opens with the creation of man, and of the Universe and of the elements; it passes in review the lives of the gods, and the marvellous feats of men of supernatural powers, such as Maui and Tawhaki, and the great achievements of the heroes of the past.[1] The programme almost invariably winds up with the arrival of a ship. This may be that of the first ancestors of the present islanders, like that which Prof. Buck witnessed in Manihiki[2] in the Pacific; or, by substitution, that of a modern European ship, such as the dramas which celebrate the arrival of Captain Cook in the Island of Mangaia[3] or that witnessed by Lamont in the Island of Penrhyn in the Pacific.[4] The ship play is enacted almost everywhere. But the whole repertoire can be traced complete in the Cook Group, as well as in Tahiti. The object of the pageant is to teach the history of the race in

1 I have given the evidence relating to the *arioi* and their performances in some detail in *The Growth of Literature*, vol. III, part II.
2 Te Rangi Hiroa (P. H. Buck), *Ethnology of Manihiki* (Honolulu, Hawaii, 1932), pp. 198 f.
3 See W. W. Gill, *Historical Sketches of Savage Life in Polynesia* (Wellington, 1880) pp. 182 ff.
4 *Wild Life among the Pacific Islanders* (London, 1867), pp. 314 ff.

the most impressive form—a combination of ritual performance with tradition. Such costly institutions are probably due to the anxiety of the *ariki* or ruling class to support their extravagant claims by commemoration of their arrival in the islands as a divine race, and under divine inspiration, the consummation of the race's history.

The importance which the Polynesians themselves attached to the educational activities of these institutions and their ritual performances is seen in the traditions which speak of their prototypes in Hawaiki, the spiritual home of the race. Here we have a detailed and complete picture of the institution of the *arioi* as it is ideally conceived. By far the most prominent feature in this ideal *whare karioi*, as it is called, is instruction—instruction in dance and song, in genealogical lore, in geographical catalogues, in the rite of tattooing, in the history of the race, and in other matters. The syllabus shows that the *arioi* institution was regarded as the principal establishment for instruction in all intellectual matters, and that the *arioi* themselves are a mobilised seasonal school, analogous to our own summer schools. It is of interest in this connection to reflect that their headquarters were in the sacred island of Raiatea, which, as I have already mentioned, was at once the principal sanctuary of the Central Pacific, and the principal repository of native scientific and historical tradition.

The conclusion to which the study of oral literature in its relationship to ritual points is that neither traditions nor ritual live long unless transmitted and enshrined in an artistic form. But the cultivation of art, such as is necessary for the handing on of tradition, is not native to poor and scattered groups, such as the lowest native civilisations are to-day. It requires the stimulus of competition, criticism, and remuneration. In the same way ritual could hardly develop in poverty and retirement. It requires wealth, specialisation, and an audience. Both imply more or less advanced political conditions and centralised populations, whether permanently centralised as in towns or great sanctuaries, or temporarily, as at religious festivals. Neither tradition nor ritual are primitive, but comparatively late growths. It is, indeed, to be suspected that the most primitive peoples living to-day are not originators, but the heirs of millennia of culture, imperfectly transmitted and now deteriorated often beyond recognition. The loftier conceptions of former civilisations are reduced to degenerate magical formulae. The development of ritual, owing to the education and tradition which are inseparable from it, has been an important factor in the development of thought. Its importance lies in its power of stimulating the imagination by radiating knowledge from the highest to the lowest.

This strong appeal to the imagination is undoubtedly the principal motive which induces the prophet, priest and seer to make extensive use of ritual. His own communion with the spirit world takes place in his own soul. But the shaman is a *psychopompos*, and the spiritual representative of his tribe. He must stimulate the imagination of his audience, however crudely, to see his own vision, to realise the truths which he himself apprehends spiritually. The sanctuary of Raiatea in the Pacific employed the *arioi* as their travelling instructors, and the islanders of Mangaia performed their poetical dramas

Plate 5. Etruscan Tomb Painting of the Dead

as a means to quicken their memories of the dead and facilitate intercourse with their spirits. The ritual of the Baganda, indeed, left nothing to the imagination, took no chances. By a master-stroke of mantic policy, it has swept into its own domain the functions of ritual, tradition, and magic, and fused them into a compelling semblance of immortality. The ecclesiastical organisation of Central Africa has aimed at nothing less than the achievement of an Earthly Paradise.

CHAPTER VI

THE SPIRITUAL JOURNEYS OF THE SEER

THE history of thought is one of the most difficult and baffling of all pursuits, even among civilised peoples who have been accustomed to preserve and circulate their thoughts in written form. It becomes a far more difficult task to trace the transmission of man's speculative and spiritual endeavour where our evidence consists of isolated patches of information—the spoken word of to-day, and a fragment of parchment from the desert sands.

In the future our main hope of unravelling the history of thought must lie in comparative literature, even the literature of areas far apart—the past with the present, the written with the oral. We cannot hope to learn the origin of the elaborate imagery and supernatural *milieu* of, for example, the Turkish tribes of Northern and Central Asia, while the MSS. of the Orkhon and of Turkestan are still buried, or studied in isolation. Again, the similarities between Siberian, Turkish and Polynesian mantic and supernatural conceptions are so close that independence is impossible. Yet racial and culture contacts are here equally impossible. We can only proceed a step at a time by studying their relationship to the nearest civilisations of the past—such as Japan, Turkestan, Java. By working back from oral to written texts we may hope to trace the chronology of mantic thought. But the starting-point must be the comparison and classification of the oral texts, and these are rapidly dis-

SPIRITUAL JOURNEYS OF THE SEER

appearing. The Russians, as we have seen, are already recruiting the Siberian shamans for the state theatre.

In Asia, in Polynesia, even in Africa, man's chief intellectual preoccupations and speculations are with spiritual adventure. A comparative study of the literary texts in which some of these adventures are treated will illustrate in some measure the contribution which oral literature can make to the history of thought. These spiritual adventures are the journeys which we take in our minds into the past, the hidden or distant present, and the future. The lonely pioneering of the soul in these spheres and the defeat or success of its quest forms the principal theme in the oral literature of the Old World.

The literary history of Europe would hardly have led us to expect this. Our most comprehensive body of literature recorded from oral tradition is the Icelandic sagas, and these are devoted to the external relations of domestic life on the grand scale. Our modern fiction is mainly concerned with social life. The term epic is now practically synonymous with narrative poetry about warlike deeds: 'I sing of arms and the man.' It is a valuable achievement of oral literature to show that this predominant preoccupation of man with himself—his almost total absorption in his temporary physical life—is a European phenomenon. And to-day it has perhaps a special refreshment and value for us to find that still, among the vast majority of mankind, the principal adventures take place, not on the field of battle, but in the mind of man.

The forms which these spiritual adventures take are many and various; but they tend to follow traditional lines. The principal themes are the journeys of mortals to the bright Heavens above, the abode of the gods; to the Underworld with its mysterious darkness, the abode of the dead; to remote and inaccessible spheres of the Universe. The Mongols and the Turkish-speaking peoples[1] and others of Central and Northern Asia have a vast epic and dramatic or liturgical literature on this theme. In Mongolia, Tibet, and Ladakh we find everywhere stories of a visit to the Underworld by the mythical king Gezar. And in Tibet to-day the lamas ceremonially conduct the souls of living men and women on preliminary excursions to the Underworld. In all these cases the similarities may be accounted for by direct contact; but it is more surprising to find that almost every group of islands in the Pacific knows the same theme, whether in saga or dramatic ritual, in mantic formula or in dirges for the dead. Whether among the Dyaks of Borneo or in Hawaii or New Zealand the greatest adventures of the greatest heroes are their journeys to the Heavens or to the abode of the dead. Everywhere these supernatural regions are populated with large and well-ordered communities, whose rulers live on a grand scale.[2]

The more immediate objects of these journeys are many and various. It may be to acquire intellectual and spiritual inspiration, to learn new arts, dances, and the gift of song and poetry—favourite motifs in Polynesia. It may be to escape from a hostile supernatural power,

[1] A detailed account of the stories and ritual referred to above, with full references, is given in my paper on 'The Spiritual Ideas and Experiences of the Tatars of Central Asia' in the *Journal of the Royal Anthropological Institute*, vol. LXVI (1936), pp. 291 ff.

[2] A detailed account of the stories and the ritual is given in my papers on 'The Kite', and 'Notes on Polynesian Mythology' in the *Journal of the Royal Anthropological Institute*, vols. LX (1930) and LXI (1931).

Plate 6. Dramatic Presentation of Yama, God of the Dead, from Choni in the Chinese Province of Kansu

to call down blessings from the supreme God of Heaven, or to take part in the life of the supernatural beings living in the skies—favourite motifs in Central and Northern Asia. But undoubtedly everywhere the principal motifs are the rescue of souls from hostile spirits, and the securing of the water of life and the herb of healing. Directly or indirectly the quest for immortality is the most outstanding motif, both in Asia and in Polynesia.

The men and women who undertake these journeys are not always professional seers or shamans. Such journeys are everywhere attributed to quite ordinary men and women. In New Zealand the English settler Shortland had a servant whose aunt made an unexpected journey to the land of the dead and returned to give a minute account of her experiences. In these expeditions the men generally require the help of supernatural beings, especially supernatural women, who are generally beneficent. But the women everywhere make the journey unaided. In Polynesia these journeys are not, I think, very often attributed to the priests, but to the gods and the great *arikis* or chiefs of the past. Where they are made by professionals to-day, as in Siberia, Tibet, and Borneo, it is generally in their capacity of *psychopompos*—the convoy of a soul. May we conclude from this that the vitality of private or individual supernatural power, or shamanism as it is generally called, is still stronger in Polynesia than in Asia?

Every effort is made by the seer or shaman to convey to his audience his experiences on these journeys in order to make them familiar with spiritual regions. Tatar shaman, Dyak manang, Tibetan lama—all take their audience with them in a kind of charade with running

94 SPIRITUAL JOURNEYS OF THE SEER

commentary, and the indelible impression which these journeys make on the lay mind can be gauged from the paramount place which they hold in the literature of entertainment. Radlov recorded a large volume of epics from the Yenisei Tatars based almost wholly on such themes.[1] From the point of view of the seer these ritual journeys are at once a means of disciplining and of informing the flock. They are an initiation into the next life. For their followers they are a kind of spiritual dress rehearsal, a trial trip to Heaven and Hell.

The distribution of our theme, then, in modern oral literature follows a great arc on the periphery of the eastern hemisphere, stretching from the Chathams in South Polynesia, round Siberia to Russia, and including the mountain masses and backward districts of Central Asia. This quest of immortality, the effort of men and women to master matter by spirit, is the chief intellectual preoccupation of the men and women outside the sphere of civilisation to-day. It is prominent also in Africa, and can be traced down the Great Rift Valley from Uganda to Zululand and up the Zambesi. Instances are too numerous to mention—Mr Sayce has called attention to many in his paper in *Folk-Lore*.[2] Shooter recorded a striking narrative of a Zulu of Chaka's court who visited the land of the dead.[3] The most outstanding is Stanley's narrative of the early Uganda king Kintu.[4] On the other hand the Basuto king Mohlomi visited the skies in a

---

1 *Proben der Volkslitteratur der Türkischen Stämme Süd-Sibiriens*, vol. II (St Petersburg, 1868).
2 *Folk-Lore*, vol. XLV, pp. 99 ff.; see especially pp. 131 .
3 *The Kafirs of Natal and the Zulu Country* (London, 1857), pp. 270 f.
4 *Through the Dark Continent* (London, 1887), pp. 218 f.

SPIRITUAL JOURNEYS OF THE SEER 95

mantic vision,[1] and King Rumanika of Karagwe also claimed to have been raised up to Heaven by supernatural means.[2] In Bantu folk-tales such mantic visions of the skies are also ascribed to women. But on the whole in Africa the ritual side of such visits of the living to the dead is more developed than its literary record or celebration.

Our theme is not confined to oral literature or to our own time. It can be traced in the *Kudatku Bilik*, a Uigur, or early eastern Turkish text written in Chinese Turkestan in 1069. Journeys of gods and heroes to the Heavens and the Underworld form the leading motif of the *Kojiki*, the earliest Japanese chronicle, which purports to have been composed in A.D. 712. These early Japanese stories show a polish of style, and a sense of the value of humour and of laughter which is rare in early written literature, and still rarer in oral literature. Its nearest equivalent in modern oral literature is found in precisely that text of the Dyaks of Borneo which deals with the same themes. This can hardly be accidental. And is it accident that in the early poetry of Scandinavia, believed to be of approximately the same period as the Japanese records, we find our closest written analogies to the early Japanese stories—journeys to the land of the dead, and stories of the gods rich in brilliant humour and humanity, and in reckless indecorum and profanity?

In Europe, however, by far the richest storehouse for these mantic journeys is to be found in the early MSS. of Ireland; but enough remains from Wales to show how rich our own Island must once have been in such themes,

[1] See Ellenberger and McGregor, *History of the Basuto* (London, 1912), p. 90.
[2] Speke, *Journal of the Discovery of the Source of the Nile*, p. 222.

and hints are not wanting even in early British and Scottish tradition.[1] Danish tradition points to a wealth of lost mantic literature of this class from all round the Baltic coasts and North Russia. Its presence in Finland is attested by many variant versions in the *Kalevala*. I suspect that some late version of the same theme lies behind Simon Grunau's remarkable Lithuanian story of the oak of Romové. And it is, I believe, to be strongly suspected that in the famous story of the funeral of the Varangian chief on the Volga recorded in the early tenth century by the Arabic traveller, Ibn Fodlan,[2] we have, not so much a literal record of actual experiences as an invaluable record of a piece of ritual and of the 'book of words' which accompanied it. It is strongly to be suspected that the 'faces of dead parents' and the 'green Paradise' referred to by the girl before she is sacrificed are ritual formulae. Suttee is unknown in Norse historical records, but the interpretation suggested above would be in perfect accord with the evidence of the ritual visit of the maiden Sigrún to the barrow in which her dead lover Helgi is interred in the early Norse Helgi poems. This ritual visit to the dead is clearly deployed in the Russian oral poem of Mikhailo Potyk and the parallel versions from the south of the Caucasus.[3]

Europe itself, then, is rich in oral traditions from the Dark Ages, recorded later in MS., which relate to mantic

[1] Certain motifs in the medieval traditions relating to Macbeth have close affinities with the early Irish visionary literature relating to the abode of the dead.
[2] The most recent translation of this invaluable narrative is that of C. Waddy in *Antiquity*, vol. VIII (1934), pp. 58 ff.
[3] See the versions cited by Dumézil, *Légendes sur les Nartes* (Paris, 1930), p. 102.

SPIRITUAL JOURNEYS OF THE SEER 97

journeys to supernatural regions and to the land of the dead. Here also they follow a periphery from the Volga through North Russia, Finland, Lithuania and the Baltic coasts, Scandinavia and the British Isles. The evidence is richest and fullest in that great oral library of mantic tradition—Irish saga. It is, therefore, especially interesting that Irish tradition persistently associates such mantic journeys with the *druids* and the *filid*, while sharing with north European and Asiatic tradition the importance attached to the female supernatural guide and guardian. From this we are led to suspect that the mantic tradition of Britain has its roots in ancient Gaul where druidism was highly developed.

The differences between medieval European and eastern mantic journeys are, however, as important as the similarities. In European oral traditional literature —apart from modern folk-tales—we have no clear examples of mortals visiting the skies. And though stories of visits to the Underworld are numerous, we have no full and sustained picture of the Underworld comparable with the Tatar and Oceanic versions. More commonly we accompany the hero or heroine or even the divine being in the flesh to the interior of the tomb, but not into the presence of the dead except as individuals. The real difference would seem to lie in the conception of the dead. In Teutonic and Celtic the dead are not generally pictured as forming very large communities, or as living in great style. Even the conception of Valhöll can, I think, be clearly demonstrated to have arisen mainly from the picture of the interior of a single barrow. The dead are, in fact, closely related to their graves, and are most commonly pictured as continuing their existence in these, rather than as joining a large community in a distant realm. But both conceptions are found both in Norse and in Celtic.

So far, then, our results show from a survey of the modern oral literature and the MS. literary records in the first millennium of our era derived from earlier oral traditions that the spiritual journeys to the land of the dead are found in a closely similar form over a great part of the northern hemisphere, forming an arc from the Chathams to Iceland and Ireland, and including parts of Africa. These traditions form the periphery of a great circle or globe, including the outlying islands and peninsulas, the northern tundras, and, more centrally, the mountain tops. They seem also once to have formed part of the cultural make-up of the vanished outlying continental civilisations, such as the Uigurs in the east, the Gauls in the west, and such intermediate communities as the commercial community on the Volga in the tenth century, partly Swedish, partly Khazar. The distribution resembles a great wheel, with the spokes converging in the south of Europe and Asia. But it will be seen that the oral traditions of to-day are confined to the more remote and backward and scattered populations, while the written records of the first millennium of our era belong for the most part to the coastal islands and peninsulas, and the more advanced communities fringing the great civilisations of the south. These form, as it were, an inner circle or stratum of our sphere.

If our conclusions are just, we ought to find in some still earlier period traces of our theme in more elaborate form among the great civilisations of the ancient world in Southern Asia and North Africa, perhaps also in

SPIRITUAL JOURNEYS OF THE SEER 99

Southern Europe. This we do indeed find.[1] The British Museum possesses a fragment of an Assyrian narrative poem relating the journey of the goddess Ishtar to the Underworld[2] to seek the soul of her son or lover Tammuz in a form strikingly similar to the modern Siberian story of Kubai-Ko recorded by the Swedish ethnographer Castrén,[3] and others recorded from the Yenisei Tatars by Radlov. In the great epic of *Gilgamesh* the supreme adventures of the hero are his mantic journey to seek immortality, and his necromantic interview with his friend Engidu. Engidu himself, before his death, visits the land of the dead in a mantic vision. Even in literary form the poem of *Gilgamesh* resembles Tatar epic poetry very closely. But most of all they resemble one another in the mingling of heroic and mantic themes, and in the easy and natural transition from the natural to the supernatural sphere. It may be said that in these two literatures, as in no other—the Assyrian and the Siberian Turkish—the distinction between mind and matter is simply non-existent; but the supreme achievements of the heroes are spiritual.

If the modern poems of the north originated in such an ancient *milieu* we must suppose the intermediate links to have perished, partly in lost civilisations, such as the Uigur. Moreover, it ought to be possible to trace at least the initial stages of such radiation in ancient Mesopotamia. This is precisely what is being done by specialists

[1] See the paper by Prof. Hooke, *Folklore*, vol. XLV, pp. 195 ff.
[2] See the *British Museum Guide to the Babylonian and Assyrian Collections* (1908), p. 44.
[3] *Nordische Reisen und Forschungen* (St Petersburg, 1853–), vols. III, pp. 148 ff.; IV, pp. 239 ff.

to-day, notably by Prof. Hooke and his colleagues,[1] and by other scholars such as the late Prof. Langdon. I may refer to the indications recently demonstrated of the spread of the myth of Marduk and of Tiamat and its traces on the literature of ancient Palestine,[2] of the fragments of literary texts of *Gilgamesh* from the Hittite area;[3] to the evidence for the cult of Tammuz in medieval Arabia. To these I would urge that we add the direct debt of Northern Europe to the Tammuz myth for the story of Balder. This story, as we have it, has no affinity or analogy in either Teutonic or Celtic myth. There is no good evidence that Balder was ever worshipped, or that he was connected with any cult.[4] His story is almost certainly intrusive. Can it be coincidence which makes his name an exact Teutonic equivalent of Adonis, Balder being the Norse equivalent of the Anglo-Saxon poetic word *Baldor*, 'lord'? It is equally significant that the two Norse stories embodying detailed accounts of a journey to the land of the dead[5] are both undertaken by gods in connection with the death of Balder, and that one of them is definitely undertaken to rescue him from the dead.

The gaps in the history of our theme can be partly bridged by material culture. The Siberian shaman in his journey to the Underworld takes his little caravan in his songs southward 'over a yellow steppe across which a magpie cannot fly',[6] and then he climbs a mountain so

[1] See especially *The Labyrinth*, a collection of essays by various scholars, ed. by Prof. Hooke (London, 1935).
[2] Hooke, *The Origins of Early Semitic Ritual* (London, 1938), pp. 37, 61.
[3] S. Langdon, 'The Sumerian Epic of Gilgamesh', *Journal of the Royal Asiatic Society*, part IV, pp. 911 ff.
[4] Despite the attractive story of the romantic *Frithjófs Saga*, ch. 1, 6.
[5] *Vegtamskvitha* and *Hermóthr's Ride to Hel*.
[6] Fuller details will be found in my paper on the 'Spiritual Ideas and Experiences of the Tatars', *op. cit.* p. 319.

Plate 7. Yama and attendant Demons in a Mystery Play from Choni in the Chinese Province of Kansu

high that the breath is drawn with difficulty, and only the bones of horses and previous dead shamans point the track. But how like the journey of the early Buddhist pilgrim Fahien! There can be no doubt that his course is pictured as leading him over the desert of Turkestan and the mountains bordering Tibet.—Many Buddhist pilgrims from Urga to Tibet could describe the route to their Kirghiz neighbours.—And having climbed, the shaman in his song and ritual dance conducts his caravan down into a hole in the ground, and what do they find? In his chanted pictures we find precisely the paraphernalia of the Buddhist caves which lie under the temples of Tibet where hideous sculptures impress on the faithful the horrors of the Underworld, and where Yama reigns supreme as the black cannibal god of the dead. But we know that these cave temples belong to the same phase of Buddhist culture as those of Turkestan and Korea in the seventh and eighth centuries, and are derived by way of Gandhara ultimately from India. Prince Erlik of the Tatar Underworld can be no other than Yama. An Altai shaman prays thus to Erlik:

> O thou mighty Erlik Khan,
> Whose hair gives forth shining sparks,
> Ever does the breast of a corpse
> Serve thee as a bowl;
> Men's skulls are thy beakers.
> Thy sword is green iron...
> Sparkling is thy black countenance.
> O Erlik, Erlik, my father,
> Why persecutest thou the people thus?
> Thy countenance is ever black as soot,
> Glittering dark like coals.[1]

Yama has declined from glory. In the Avesta of ancient

[1] Radlov, *Proben*, vol. v, p. 471 f.

Persia he is Adam and Noah combined—the survivor from the flood and the progenitor of the human race—surely very close to Uta-napishtim of *Gilgamesh*.

The system of radiation which seems to account for the mantic journeys of the oral literature of Asia and Polynesia does not wholly account for those of Europe and Africa. In ancient Greek literature the myth of Demeter and Persephone and the *nekuia* of Homer belong to the Asiatic group; and in later times it is difficult to dissociate Druidism and the philosophy and religion of ancient Thrace from the Brahmins of India. On the other hand the story of the Thracian seer Salmoxis[1] is strikingly similar to Speke's account of Dagara, father of King Rumanika in Karagwe on the Victoria Nyanza.[2] The transformations attributed to them, and their underground sojourn are more suggestive of Uganda, the Baganda mediums and the Uganda tombs than of the ritual for the dead in Asia and Polynesia. And we have seen that in general Teutonic and Celtic visits to the Underworld are more closely associated with the burial chamber than those of Asia and Polynesia. Are these early European and modern African motifs offshoots from a common stock with a western origin, possibly in Egypt? Can any lost links be traced, e.g. in the Greek mysteries, in ancient Thracian practice, and in the early Etruscan tomb paintings? The latter show us the journey of the soul to the abode of the dead under convoy of a winged spirit—a *psychopompos* like the shaman of Siberia on his bird, and then in his feather coat, and the Irish *filid* with their cloaks trimmed with birds' feathers.

1 Herodotus, IV, 96.
2 Speke, *op. cit.* p. 235.

SPIRITUAL JOURNEYS OF THE SEER 103

In Europe at any rate the evidence of early written literature makes it clear that the currents from south to north have alternated with currents from east to west. In early Norse poems and saga we find a supernatural maiden Kara, who bears a close resemblance to the supernatural maiden Kara Chach in the Kirghiz poem of Er Töschtük.[1] Is this one of a number of unrecognised Turkish contributions to Norse literature? The name Kara (cf. Turk. 'black') and the rôle she plays are unique in Norse. But her functions are widespread in Turkish oral poetry, and her name recalls the Turkish word *kara*. Kara must have come across the steppe and up the Volga. The kumiss-drinking, horse-racing Este in East Prussia referred to in King Alfred's version of Wulfstan's voyage show an aristocracy from the steppe in North-Eastern Europe in the ninth century. The accident of our possessing an earlier Chronicle for South Russia than for the North has obscured the importance of early Turkish movements to North-Western Russia. But this blank is certainly capable of being made good to a considerable extent by a critical use of the Norse sagas, especially those of Swedish provenance. Even Beowulf's flying dragon has many relatives in the first degree in North-Western Russia and Finland, and they must have flown there straight from the steppe. They belong to the same ancestral stock as Tugarín Fiery Dragon of the Russian oral narrative poems, who has been identified with the great Tatar chief Tugor Khan, whose daughter was married to Vladimir Monomakh, prince of Kiev, in 1094.

It is not difficult to visualise a chronological scheme

[1] Radlov, *Proben*, vol. v, pp. 530 ff.

for the history of mantic thought relating to the Underworld; but the history and chronology of the journeys to the Heavens are more difficult, owing to the fact that for these journeys there is relatively little material in early written records; though in the great Indian epic the *Mahabharata*,[1] the hero Arjuna visits Heaven in the chariot of Indra. Again material culture has some help for us. The cult of kite-flying in the Pacific[2] is closely related to that of the bird on the steppe, and this is undoubtedly old. We meet it in Turkish inscriptions on the Orkhon at least as early as the eighth century A.D., and in the temple of Zeus at Dodona many centuries before; and in *Gilgamesh* are not the dead pictured as clad in birds' feathers? The distribution of the cult of the soul under the form of a bird coincides in general with that of the mantic journey to the Heavens.

Our brief survey suggests that the spiritual adventures of man are moulded by the traditional spiritual experiences of the past. His excursions into the speculative world follow ancient routes, trodden long ago by spiritual thinkers of other regions. Local conditions and personal impulse will prompt and modify and recreate the imaginative effort of a tohunga, or a shaman, or a druid; but the routes along which his imagination can travel, and the baggage which his little caravan can carry have been determined elsewhere long ago in Erech and in Thebes. Their routes have passed, some through the

1 *Mahabharata*, book III, ch. 42. Here Indra's charioteer who comes down from Heaven for the hero Arjuna is probably the forerunner of the groom who goes to Heaven with the Altai Shaman.
2 I have given a detailed survey of this practice in the Pacific and of the stories associated with it in my paper on 'The Kite'. See p. 92 above.

ancient Hindu kingdoms of Java; through the buried cities of Chinese Turkestan; the ruined cities of Etruria, the long forgotten Khazar emporium of Itill on the Volga. Both in east and west the journeys to the Underworld appear to be older than those to the Heavens. And this is in accordance with the widely held view that in Siberia black shamanism is earlier than white, as it is undoubtedly more widespread. It is also in accordance with the Polynesian tradition that the earliest hero Maui failed to achieve immortality by his journey through the regions of darkness, while the later hero Tawhaki achieved it by his journey to the Heavens. The great Assyrian epic itself is the record of a failure to achieve immortality by following the traditional cult of the dead. It is not easy to account for the temple prestige which this theme enjoyed unless it is as a piece of religious propaganda by those who wished to discredit it and to substitute a new cult—that of immortality to be achieved by gods not of the Underworld.

INDEX

African manticism, 40
Ajanta, cave temples of, 82
Alcestis, 60
Alfred, King, 3, 103
Allen, Battle of, 10
Altai shaman, 82
Altai Tatars, 16, 52, 59
Amargin, 5, 54
Anadirsk, 19
Ankole, 77
Ariki, 80, 87, 93
Arioi, 25, 85, 86, 87, 88
Arioi of Tahiti, dramatic poetry of, 50
Arjuna, 104
Ashe, Rev. R. P., 35
Aşoka, King, 82
Asser, Bishop, 4
Atete, feast of, 74
Atuas, 21, 23
Avesta, 101

Babylonian Epic of Creation, 82
Baganda, 33, 34, 35, 77, 89
Baker, Sir Samuel, 32
Baksha, 18, 20
Balder, 100
Bali, Island of, 78, 80, 81
Basuto, initiation ceremonies of the young, 31
Bede, Venerable, 3
Beowulf, 4
Beowulf's flying dragon, 103
'Birds of Rhiannon', 59 *n*.
Black Book of Carmarthen, 4 *n*.
Bogoras, 19
Bön priests of Tibet, 19
Borneo, 93
Bósi, 9
Brahmins, 12, 44
British Museum, 99
Buck, Prof. P. H., 86
Buddhist Central Asia, oral literature of, 27

Buryat, 17, 20; religious beliefs, 76

Caedmon, 3, 4
Calchas, 2
Calchas and Mopsos, 48
Carmelites, 67, 68, 69
Casalis, E., 31
Castagné, J., 18, 28 *n*., 46 *n*., 53
Castrén, M. A., 3, 99
Cave temples, 82
Celtic literature, 6
Celtic manticism, 6
Chaka's court, a Zulu of, 94
Charms, 79, 84
Chatham Islands, 81, 94, 98
Chuckchee shaman, utterances of, 70
Cicero, 11
Contemplative elements in Norse literature, 65, 66
Cook, Captain, 86
Cook Group, 53, 86
Corc, 54
Creation, Babylonian Epic of, 82
Cynewulf, 4

Dagara, 102
Dante, 70
Dead, conception of the, 97; journey to land of the, 100
Deities, the *mandwas* of zoomorphic, 33, 34
Delphic oracle, 41
Demeter and Persephone, myth of, 102
Devil-dances, 34
Diviciacus, 11
Dramas, ritual, 25
Dream of the Cross, The, 4
Druids, 12
Drum, use of in ritual dramas, 24, 25
Dyak manang, 93
Dyaks of Borneo, 92, 95

INDEX

Ecstasy, regulation of, 58
Eggthér, 7
Egill Skallagrímsson, 76
Ellenberger, F. W., 30
Emin Pasha, 32
Engidu, 99
Erech, 104
Erlik, Prince, 101
Er Töschtük, 103
Etruria, 105
Exeter Book, 4

Fahien, 101
Felkin, Rev. R. W., 35
Finn, 54
Flateyjarbók, 9
Folklore, 94
Frazer, Sir J. G., 85 n.
Funeral practices, 80

Galdrar, 8
Galla of East Africa, 74
Gandhara, 82, 101
Gauls, 98
Geilt, Suibhne, 50
Genealogical lore, 79
Gezar, mythical king, 92
Gilgamesh, 57
Gilgamesh, 83, 99, 100, 102, 104
Gill, W. W., 22 n., 23, 24
Gmelin, 18
Grant, J. A., 32
Great Rift Valley, 94
Grimbold, 4
Grunau, Simon, 96
Guest, Lady Charlotte, 7 n.
Gunnwald, 7
Guthmundr, King, 9, 56
Gwawd, 13

Halfdan the Black, 7
Hallfrethar Saga, 7
Harold Hardrada, Icelandic saga of, 83
Harold the Fair-haired, King of Norway, 7, 9 n.
Hawaii, 25, 92
Hawaiki, 87

Heaven, journey to, 16, 17, 104
Heithr, 9
Heithrekr and Othin, riddle contest between, 49
Helgi, 96
Herrauthr and Bósi, Saga of, 9
Hesiod, 2, 50
Hild, Abbess, 3
Hildén, K., 52
Hoki, 85
Homer, 102
Hooke, Prof., 10c
Hróaldr, 7
Hud, 13
Hud-lath, 13

Ibn Fodlan, 96
Iceland, 98; magic in, 75
Iliad, 2
Ilighin, 18
Indra, 104
Inspiration, 21, 41, 42
Interior Castle, The, 67, 68
Ishtar, 60, 99
Itill, 105

Japan, 90
Japanese oral literature, 95
Java, 90, 105
Jenghiz Khan, 71
Jones, Sir John Morris, 5 n.

Kagwa, Sir Apolo, 34, 37, 61 n.
Kalevala, 96
Kamlanie, 16
Kanishka, King, 82
Kara, 103
Kara Chach, 103
Karagwe, 102
Karakias, 78
Katikiro, 37
Katsina (Emir of), 46 n.
Kaulas, 25
Kava, 22 n., 58
Kazak-Kirghiz, 53
Kennan, G., 19, 76
Khingan Tungus, 52
Khorkoutt, 28 n.

INDEX

Khorro, 18
Kigala, King, 38
Kintu, King, 94
Kirghiz Tatars, 82
Klieng, 85
Kobuz, 28 n.
Kögel-Khan, 3
Kojiki, 27, 95
Kolyma, river, 18
Korean cave temples, 82
Koryak, 18, 19
Kotkell, 8
Kshatriya, 80
Kubai-Ko, 99
Kudatku Bilik, 95
Kura, sagas of, 53

Ladakh, 92
Lamont, E. H., 86
Langdon, Prof., 100
Laxdaela Saga, 8
Lindgren, Miss E. J., 15 n., 17, 18, 41, 46 n.
Livingstone, David, 29, 30
Luganda, 37

Mabinogion, 7 n.
MacAirt, Cormac, High-king of Ireland, 50, 59 n.
Maelgwn, Court of, 4
Magic, 74, 75, 81, 82
Mahabharata, 55, 76, 104
Manannan mac Lír, 10
Mandwa, 32, 33, 37, 38, 57
Mangaia, 22, 86, 88; ritual dramatic poetry of, 49
Mangaian 'fairies', 23
Manganja, 29
Mangareva, 54
Manihiki, 86
Mantic poetry, 5
Mantic thought, 90
Mantic visions, 95
Manticism, 11, 12, 52, 55, 56, 57, 59, 60; and Shamanism, link between, 12
Maori New Zealand, magic in, 75

Marduk, 100
Marquesas, 21, 22, 85; chanting of genealogies, 79
Maui, 80, 81, 86, 105; sagas of, 53
Mautara, priest of Motoro, 24 n.
'Memory', mother of the Muses, 2
Merlin, 50
Mikhailo Potyk, 96
Mimir, head of, 50
Mohlomi, 30, 50, 94
Monastic Orders, 66
Mongan, King, 5
Mongolia, 92
Mongols, 92
Mopsos, 2
Morann, 54
Moriori of the Chatham Islands, 79
Moshesh, 30
Motoro, priests of, 22, 24
Muses, the, 2, 84
Music, use of, 14, 45; and singing, 1–9

New Zealand, 92
Ngati-Vara, 24
Niemojowski, 53
No plays of Japan, 55
Nornagestr, 8, 9

Óddinsakr, 'the land of immortals', 9, 10
Odyssey, 2, 60
Olaf Tryggvason, Saga of, 8
Oral traditions, 98
Orkhon, 90, 104
Örvar-Odds Saga, 9
Ostyak, 20
Othin, 9, 10, 55, 56, 59
Óthrerir, 13

Pele, 25; priestesses of, 21, 22
Penrhyn, Island of, 86
Perham, Ven. Archdeacon, 26 n.
Persephone, 60
Poetic inspiration, mantic, 2, 5, 20, 22, 69

INDEX

Polynesia, 77, 78
Praetorius, Matthaeus, 12
Psychopompos, 88, 93, 102
Pwyll, 8

Radlov, W. W., 3 *n*., 47, 94, 99
Raiatea, sanctuary of, 25, 74, 87, 88
Rarotonga, Island of, 23, 53, 80
Romové, the story of the oak of, 96
Rongo, 23
Roscoe, Rev. J., 34, 35, 36, 37, 38, 39, 44
Rumanika, King of Karagwe, 95, 102
Runic inscribed monument, 7

Saga, Irish, 97; Norse, 103; religious, 83
Sagas, Icelandic, 91
Sages, contests between, 48
Saitas, 13
Salmoxis, 102
Sandschejew, 44, 51
Saxo Grammaticus, 56
Sayce, A. H., 94
Schagai, 51
Sea Dyaks, 27, 46, 78, 84; oral literature of, 26
Seer, 30; 'call' of the, Carmelite evidence, 67; the function of, 14. *See also* Shamans
Seithr, 13
Seith-stafr, 13
Seligman, C. G. and B. Z., 21
Selwanga, 33
Shakespeare, 84
Shaman, a *psychopompos*, 88; 'call' of a, 51
Shamaness, 'call' of a, 51; dance of a, 17, 18
Shamanism and manticism, link between, 12
Shamans, 9 *n*., 10, 15; costume and equipment of, 58; and divine spirit, 62; ecstasy, 62, 63; mentally healthy, 65; ritual, 73; training of, 52, 53, 54; trance of the, 16

Ship play, 86
Shirokogoroff, 64, 65 *n*.
Shooter, J., 30, 94
Siberia, 93, 94
Sieroszewski, 9 *n*., 73
Sigrún, 96
Singalang Burong, 84, 85
Smith, S. Percy, 44 *n*., 53
Snoldelev, Denmark, 7
Snorri, 75
Snorri Sturluson, 7 *n*.
Soma, 58
Song of the Dyak Head Feast, The, 78, 84
Speke, Capt. J. H., 33, 102
Spells, singing of, 8
Spiritual adventures, 91, 92, 93
Stadling, J., 47, 71
Stanley, H. M., 94

Tahiti, 22, 86
Talhaern, 4
Taliesin, 4, 5, 54
Tammuz, 99, 100
Tane, 23
Tangaroa, 85
Tat aguen, 'Father of poetry', 4
Tatar shaman, ritual of, 81
Tatars, oral literature of the, 2, 8, 71
Tautiti, 25
Tawhaki, 79, 80, 81, 82, 86, 105
Teiresias, 60
Teresa, Life of St, 68
Teresa, St, 66, 67, 68, 69, 70
Thebes, 104
Thomas Aquinas, St, 70
Thor, 9
Thorfinns Saga Karlsefnis, 8, 9, 58
Thorleifr the Wise, 7
Thrace, Manticism in, 11
Tiamat, 100
Tibet, 82, 92, 93, 101; cave temples in, 82, 101
Tir Tairngaire, 59 *n*.
Tlapone, 30
Tohungas, 79

Trevandrum, 80
Triads, Welsh, 5
Trondhjem, 83
Tugarín Fiery Dragon, 103
Tugor Khan, 103
Turkestan, 90
Tydain, 5

Uganda, 77, 94, 102; official manticism in, 32
Uigurs, 98, 99
Uigurs of Turkestan, cave temples of, 82
Underworld, journey to the, 16, 82, 97, 99, 100, 102, 105
Ungin Shaman Ucha, 51
Urga, 101
Uta-napishtim, 102

Valhöll, 97
Vedda shamans, 21

Vladimir Monomakh, 103
Völuspá, 7
Völva, 9, 10

Wanana, 42, 46
Way of Perfection, The, 68
Whare karioi, 87
Whitby, monastic life at, 3
Wimmer, L. F. A., 7 *n.*
Wulfstan, 103

Yakut, 17, 19, 20; shaman, 82
Yama, 101
Yenisei Ostyak, 17
Yenisei Tatars, 60, 82, 94, 99
Yukaghir, 19
Yurak, 17, 20

Zambesi, 94
Zeus, temple of, at Dodona, 104
Zululand, 94